KINGS AND PROPHETS

THE BIBLE
AND
ITS STORY

1

THE CREATION

2

THE PATRIARCHS
AND MOSES

3

IN THE PROMISED LAND

4

KINGS AND PROPHETS

5

EXILE AND RETURN

6

JESUS THE CHRIST

7

THE LORD'S FOLLOWERS

Planned and produced by
Jaca Book—Le Centurion
from the ideas of
Charles Ehlinger, Hervé Lauriot Prévost,
Pierre Talec, and the editorial committee
of Jaca Book

A chapter outline for this volume
is printed on the last two pages
of the volume.

KINGS AND PROPHETS

THE BIBLE AND ITS STORY

Text by Enrico Galbiati, Elio Guerriero, Antonio Sicari
Translation by Kenneth D. Whitehead
Illustrations by Antonio Molino

Winston Press   430 Oak Grove   Minneapolis, Minnesota 55403

Published in Italy under the title
Re E Profeti
Copyright © 1983 Jaca Book—Le Centurion

**Licensed publisher and distributor
of the English-language edition:**
Winston Press, Inc.
430 Oak Grove
Minneapolis, Minnesota 55403
United States of America

Agents:
Canada—
LeDroit/Novalis-Select
135 Nelson Street
Ottawa, Ontario
Canada K1N 7R4

Australia, New Zealand, New Guinea, Fiji Islands—
Dove Communications, Pty. Ltd.
Suite 1 60-64 Railway Road
Blackburn, Victoria 3130
Australia

Winston Scriptural Consultant:
Catherine Litecky, CSJ
Department of Theology
College of St. Catherine
St. Paul, Minnesota

Winston Staff:
Lois Welshons, Hermann Weinlick—editorial
Reg Sandland, Kathe Wilcoxon—design

Jaca Book—Le Centurion Editorial Committee:
François Brossier, Maretta Campi, Charles Ehlinger,
Enrico Galbiati, Elio Guerriero, Pierre Talec

Color selection: Carlo Scotti, Milan
Printing: Gorenjski tisk, Kranj, Yugoslavia

Library of Congress Catalog Card Number: 83-60313
ISBN: 0-86683-194-0

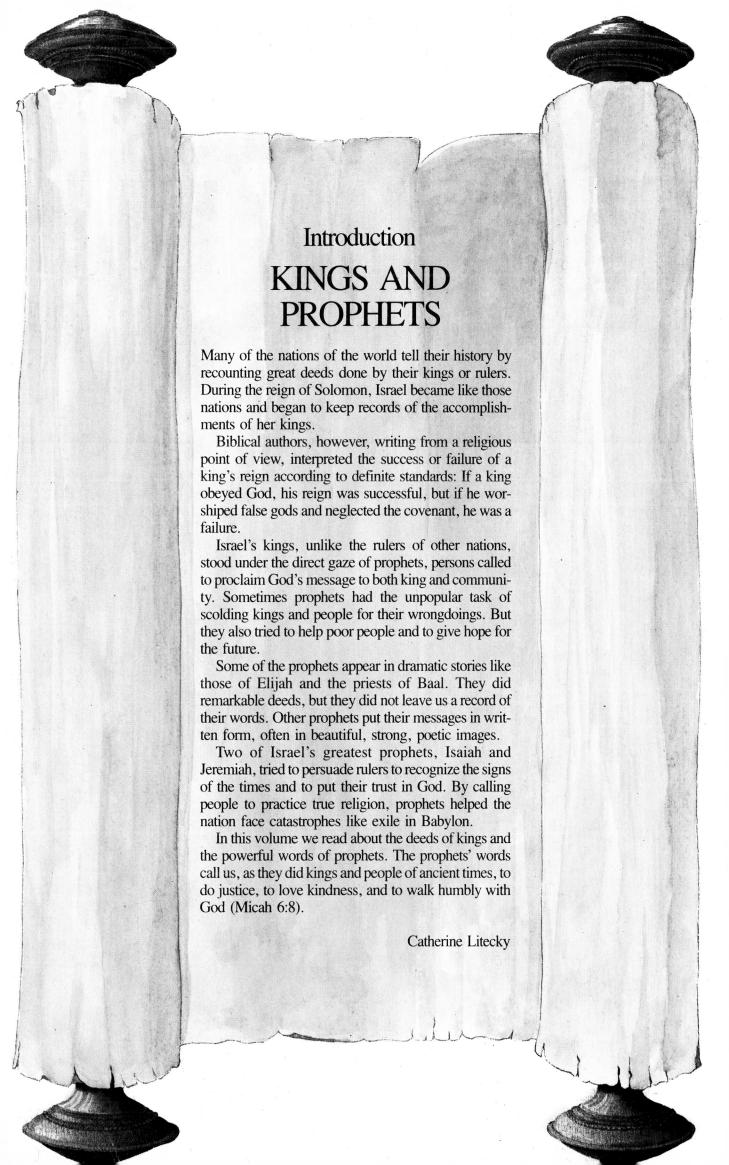

Introduction

KINGS AND PROPHETS

Many of the nations of the world tell their history by recounting great deeds done by their kings or rulers. During the reign of Solomon, Israel became like those nations and began to keep records of the accomplishments of her kings.

Biblical authors, however, writing from a religious point of view, interpreted the success or failure of a king's reign according to definite standards: If a king obeyed God, his reign was successful, but if he worshiped false gods and neglected the covenant, he was a failure.

Israel's kings, unlike the rulers of other nations, stood under the direct gaze of prophets, persons called to proclaim God's message to both king and community. Sometimes prophets had the unpopular task of scolding kings and people for their wrongdoings. But they also tried to help poor people and to give hope for the future.

Some of the prophets appear in dramatic stories like those of Elijah and the priests of Baal. They did remarkable deeds, but they did not leave us a record of their words. Other prophets put their messages in written form, often in beautiful, strong, poetic images.

Two of Israel's greatest prophets, Isaiah and Jeremiah, tried to persuade rulers to recognize the signs of the times and to put their trust in God. By calling people to practice true religion, prophets helped the nation face catastrophes like exile in Babylon.

In this volume we read about the deeds of kings and the powerful words of prophets. The prophets' words call us, as they did kings and people of ancient times, to do justice, to love kindness, and to walk humbly with God (Micah 6:8).

Catherine Litecky

Greeks

Egyptians

1 Peoples of the Near East around 1000 B.C.

Israelites
During King Solomon's reign—between 970 and 931 B.C.—the unified kingdom of Israel with its capital in Jerusalem reached the height of its splendor and strength. Even then, however, there was still some discontent and rivalry among the tribes. The powerful tribes of Ephraim and Manasseh in the north felt special resentment toward Judah. Disputes were usually settled in favor of Judah, the tribe of the royal family. These tribal rivalries, added to heavy taxes and forced labor, eventually caused a split into two kingdoms.

Arameans
During Solomon's reign this people invaded northern Mesopotamia and Syria. Two Aramean kingdoms, Damascus and Zoba, sprang up on the northern borders of Solomon's kingdom, and for a time they were subject to Israel. Later, Damascus became Israel's very strong enemy.

Phoenicians
By this time, Phoenicia was free of Egyptian domination. The Phoenicians exported their dyes and the cedars of Lebanon and engaged in far-reaching sea trade. They formed an association of city-states, each with its own king. Tyre was the most powerful Phoenician city-state in this period. King Hiram of Tyre, a friend of Solomon's, furnished both materials and workmen for Solomon's lavish program of construction in Jerusalem.

Phoenicians

Assyrians

Arameans

Israelites

Jerusalem

Assyrians

Assyria, which had been a great empire earlier, was not a strong military force during Solomon's reign. In fact, Assyria even lost some conquered territories. It was only under Ashurdan II (932-910 B.C.) that a new wave of Assyrian conquests began. Two centuries later the northern kingdom of Israel fell to Assyrian conquest.

Greeks

The glory of the Mycenaean civilization (about 1600-1100 B.C.) had faded by the time Solomon reigned. Greece was in a period of transition while a new civilization was developing. By this time, the islands of the Aegean Sea as well as the coasts of Asia Minor had been settled by Greeks. There the legends of the Greek heroes were already taking shape. These legends would later be told in the poetry of the *Iliad* and the *Odyssey*.

Egyptians

The reign of Solomon occurred at the same time that Egypt's power was declining under the twenty-first dynasty (1085-935 B.C.). The last pharaoh of this dynasty gave one of his daughters as a wife to Solomon. Pharaoh Sheshonk I, called Shishak in the Bible, began the twenty-second dynasty (935-729 B.C.). After Solomon died, this pharaoh raided Judah and destroyed Jerusalem.

2 Solomon, king following David,
asked God for the wisdom
to rule well.
God also granted him wealth,
peace, and long life.
A story about Solomon
and two arguing women
demonstrates his wisdom.

When David was an old man, he decided to choose his successor from among his sons. Passing the kingship to the firstborn son was not the custom in ancient Israel. The king could choose the son he loved most and thought most capable of governing, even if he was the youngest son. This was the case with Solomon.

To avoid trouble after he died—and trouble already was brewing—David had Solomon proclaimed and consecrated king while he himself was still alive. Then, as Scripture says, the aged king died "at a ripe old age, wealthy and respected" (2 Chronicles 29:28).

In spite of the efforts David had made to keep the peace, Solomon's reign began with some violence. In those days, it was often necessary to do away with some enemies within court in order to hold on to the throne. Solomon took quick action to rid himself of opponents.

Even so, the reign of Solomon—as we shall see in later chapters—was a period of great peace and prosperity in Israel. The fame of the young king spread far and wide among the neighboring kingdoms. He was famous for his wisdom; he had excellent judgment; and he knew how to govern.

There was one particularly important incident in the first years of Solomon's reign. It occurred at Gibeon, where Solomon had gone to offer sacrifices to the Lord. As usual, Solomon's offerings were very generous. Later in the evening, as he slept, he had a vision. He dreamed that God came to him and asked, "What should I give you?" Solomon replied,

"O Lord God, you have let me succeed my father as king, even though I am very young and don't know how to rule. Here I am among the people you have chosen to be your own, a people who are so many that they cannot be counted. So give me the wisdom I need to rule your people with justice and to know the difference between good

There is one especially well-known story about Solomon's wisdom. One day two women came before Solomon for his judgment in a dispute they were having. One of them held a baby in her arms that the other woman said was hers. The situation was confusing. It seems that the two women lived in the same place, and both had given birth to new babies at about the same time. One of these babies had died during the night. Now in front of the king, each woman cried out and claimed to be the mother of the live baby.

The king observed the women very closely. Obviously, one of the two did not want to accept the death of her own baby and was jealous of the other whose baby had lived. But which one was the real mother?

Solomon commanded the women to stop arguing. Then he called to one of his soldiers and said, "Divide the living child in two, and give half to the one, and half to the other" (1 Kings 3:25). The king knew that the true mother would rebel at such a horror.

One woman immediately said, "Please don't kill the baby! Give it to her!" And the other woman—the angry, jealous one whose child had died—replied, "Don't give it to either of us; go on and cut it in two" (1 Kings 3:26 TEV).

Thus it was clear in the eyes of all the people who was the true mother; she was the one who loved her baby so much that she was willing to give it up in order to save the child's life. She had made this decision even though she would suffer as a result.

The people of Israel marveled that God had given Solomon such wisdom to settle disputes fairly. Solomon's fame spread.

and evil. Otherwise, how would I ever be able to rule this great people of yours?"

(1 Kings 3:7-9 TEV)

God communicated with Solomon through this unusual dream. God was very pleased that Solomon had not asked for either a long life, or wealth, or power—all quite natural requests. Instead, Solomon had asked for the wisdom to govern his people well. So God said to Solomon,

"I will do what you have asked. I will give you more wisdom and understanding than anyone has ever had before or will ever have again. I will also give you what you have not asked for: all your life you will have wealth and honor, more than that of any other king. And if you obey me and keep my laws and commands, as your father David did, I will give you a long life." (1 Kings 3:12-14 TEV)

God did, in fact, grant all these gifts to Solomon during his lifetime.

3 During Solomon's reign
of peace and prosperity,
Israel's government
was well organized,
foreign trade grew,
and neighboring nations paid
tribute money to Israel.

Solomon inherited from David a kingdom that was at peace both within itself and with its neighbors. Israel had not only defeated its enemies, but had made them into tribute-paying subjects. Solomon collected tribute from the subject peoples along Israel's borders, and he also collected from the Arameans of Syria. Also, he controlled all the trade routes between the Gulf of Aqaba and the Euphrates River and collected a tax on all goods passing through. So Israel was more than a single kingdom; it was also an empire of sorts, in which various peoples recognized Solomon's authority over them.

Solomon made his administration of the kingdom more efficient by dividing the whole territory (excluding Judah) into twelve administrative regions, or districts. These districts, fairly equal in population and crop production, did not all correspond to the traditional tribal divisions. Each district had to provide enough food and other necessities to maintain Solomon's large, luxurious court for one month of every year. In each district was an officer

who was in charge of gathering food from farmers and shepherds. The twelve district officers reported to a chief officer who had charge of all the court.

Another new thing Solomon did—which didn't please his people, who were used to a life of fields and flocks—was to recruit thousands of men for forced labor away from home. This labor was necessary to carry out the king's building projects. In addition to building the Temple and the royal palace in Jerusalem, Solomon also rebuilt and fortified the principal cities. He did this partly for military reasons and partly so that each city or town would have granaries and storehouses for the food and other necessities needed by the royal court.

Still another change Solomon made was in his foreign trade policy. This trade was not left to individual merchants but was managed by the officers of the king. Solomon constructed a port at Ezion-geber, or Elath, on the Gulf of Aqaba. There he fitted out a fleet of ships with the help of his friend Hiram, king of Tyre, who provided Phoenician shipbuilders and

sailors. This fleet sailed the Red Sea, calling at ports in southern Arabia and East Africa, and returning with gold from Ophir and other rare merchandise. They probably even brought back items from as far away as India, including such things as ivory, precious stones, and even live monkeys.

Solomon also traded in war chariots, which he had purchased in Egypt in order to resell them in Syria and Asia Minor. And he also developed horse breeding. He bought horses in Cilicia in Asia Minor and kept them in the numerous stables he had at Hazor and Megiddo, as well as in the capital. The horses were bred and resold in Egypt and other neighboring countries.

Under Solomon, the lives of many Israelites were made better in many ways. They were proud of Solomon's fame and the splendor of his court; they enjoyed years of peace and prosperity. But it was also during this period that for the first time a noticeable gap appeared between the rich and the poor in Israel.

4 Solomon built a magnificent temple for God and a royal palace for himself. He used workers and materials from both Israel and neighboring nations.

To the north of Jerusalem's most ancient walls arose a hill that David earlier had purchased for the construction of a Temple. By building an outer wall around the hill, Solomon joined it to the existing city, and on it he built both the Temple and his royal palace.

Work on the Temple began in the fourth year of Solomon's reign (around 965 B.C.); it took seven years to complete. Work on the royal palace took thirteen years. Skilled woodworkers were provided by Hiram, king of Tyre. Solomon recruited forced labor among the Israelites to work alongside Phoenicians in cutting down the cedars and spruce trees of

Lebanon. The logs were taken down to the sea and tied together to make rafts that were then floated down to the port of Joppa. There some preliminary work was done on this wood, and then it was transported to Jerusalem, to be used for beams, girders, doors, and inside wall construction. The outer Temple walls were made of stone quarried locally in Judah by thousands of stonecutters.

The inside of the Temple was about forty yards in length; it was divided into three sections by partitions made out of cedar. On both sides of the outside door stood two huge columns of bronze about ten yards high. Just inside the door, there was a vestibule, or entryway, about five yards deep.

A massive quadrangular door led into a larger room called "the Holy," which was about twelve by twenty-four yards in area. This room was finished with cedar panels that were carved with floral patterns and richly gilded. It contained a small altar of gold, on which incense was burned; ten golden candlesticks; and a table overlaid with gold and with gold furnishings on which "the Bread of the Presence" was placed. There were twelve loaves of such bread, recalling the twelve tribes of Israel. The room was lighted by windows placed near the ceiling.

A pentagon-shaped door, covered with a veil woven out of gold threads, led from "the Holy" into a room called "the Holy of Holies." This inner sanctuary, about twelve yards by twelve, was completely dark inside. The "Holy of Holies" contained two cherubim—winged figures seen often in art of the ancient Near East. These cherubim were made out of olive wood overlaid with gold. The cherubim's wings touched one another and formed a kind of canopy under which rested the ark of the covenant, which contained the tables of the Law. The ark had been the most sacred object in Israel from the time of Moses on; it symbolized the presence of the invisible God in the midst of the people.

Against the outside walls, on the sides and the back of the Temple, a three-storied addition was built; this addition contained storerooms.

The Temple building was surrounded by a courtyard for the priests. In it was an altar for the holocausts (burnt offerings) and a bronze basin for ablutions (washings for purification) that was held up by twelve bronze bulls. Another outer courtyard, which connected with the royal palace, served for assemblies of the people. The nearby royal palace was constructed with the same magnificence as the Temple.

5 The ark of the covenant,
the sign of the presence of God,
was carried by the priests
into the most holy room
of the Temple,
called the Holy of Holies.
Solomon thanked God
for the covenant with Israel and
asked for God's continued help.

When the Temple was finished, it was time to place in it the ark of the covenant, which some years earlier David had brought into Jerusalem.

Solomon gathered the people together for a festival. Sacrifices of countless sheep and oxen were offered to God, and then a long procession was organized. The priests carried the ark of the covenant into the sacred inner sanctuary of the Temple, "the Holy of Holies." After everyone went out, even the priests, a cloud filled the Temple. From the time of the Exodus, the cloud had been a sign of the presence of God. The cloud's appearance at this time showed the people that God was pleased by the construction of a dwelling for himself.

Then Solomon spoke to all the people. He blessed God and praised him for carrying out all his promises. He reminded the people that it was the Lord who had decided that the Temple would be built not by David but by David's heir. He expressed his gratitude to God for having been allowed to build this majestic Temple.

After that, Solomon prayed a long prayer to the Lord. In his prayer Solomon above all thanked God for the covenant which God had made with his father David and with himself. He asked God to be merciful, to carry out all his promises, and always to be with the people in his Temple. Then he prayed,

"But can you, O God, really live on earth? Not even all of heaven is large enough to hold you, so how can this Temple that I have built be large enough? Lord my God, I am your servant. Listen to my prayer, and grant the requests I make to you today. Watch over this Temple day and night, this place where you have chosen to be worshiped. Hear me when I face this Temple and pray."

(1 Kings 8:27-29 TEV)

Finally, Solomon prayed to God for all those who would ever come to pray in this holy place, asking God to judge the guilty and save the innocent. He asked God to grant pardon for sin and help in times of defeat. He begged God to let the Temple be a place of refuge and intercession in times of famine, drought, or other calamity. The king prayed,

"If any of your people Israel, out of heartfelt sorrow, stretch out their hands in prayer toward this Temple, hear their prayer. Listen to them in your home in heaven, forgive them, and help them. You alone know the thoughts of the human heart." (1 Kings 8:38-39 TEV)

In his prayer, King Solomon even looked ahead to a time when foreign pilgrims who did not belong to the Chosen People would come to the Temple in Jerusalem to find the true God and seek salvation from him. They would come because they had heard about the God of Israel. God would hear the prayers even of such strangers—until his name became known throughout all the earth. Solomon prayed that the people could still turn towards the Temple and ask for God's pardon even if the worst should happen to them—even if the people were vanquished and deported to a strange land.

At the end of his prayer, Solomon turned back to the people and blessed them, exercising a priestly power that the Israelites recognized in their kings. He told the people always to fulfill their obligations towards God and to recognize and accept his grace. "Let your heart . . . be wholly true to the Lord our God, walking in his statutes and keeping his commandments" (1 Kings 8:61).

The feast for the dedication of the Temple lasted for seven days. Then everyone returned home.

Appearing again to Solomon, the Lord assured him that he had heard his prayer. The Lord said to Solomon:

"If you will serve me in honesty and integrity, as your father David did, and if you obey my laws and do everything I have commanded you, I will keep the promise I made to your father David when I told him that Israel would always be ruled by his descendants." (1 Kings 9:4-5 TEV)

6 Through trade, diplomacy, and
marriage to a princess of Egypt,
as well as his armies,
Solomon became a strong ruler.
The queen of Sheba came and
brought many gifts to Solomon.
Like other visitors,
she was impressed by Solomon
and his kingdom.

King Solomon kept his country safe by maintaining
its military strength. He reorganized the army, and
he situated it in well-supplied forts around the
country.

Solomon, however, did not try to conquer other
countries by violent means. Instead, he built up his
importance by developing diplomatic and trade relations with other countries. His reputation eventually
became so great that he was able to unite his house
with that of the pharaoh of Egypt; he married one of
pharaoh's daughters, something that had been considered impossible up to then for the ruler of a state
like Israel.

Solomon also maintained good relations with Hiram, king of Tyre. Hiram helped him build the fleet that enabled him to trade with Arabia and East Africa; he also supplied Solomon both with gold and with spruce and cedar wood for the construction of the Temple and royal palace.

All in all, Solomon was the most powerful ruler in the entire area that stretched between the Euphrates and the borders of Egypt; he dominated the other smaller kingdoms in the area. Never again after Solomon was Israel able to achieve the level of well-being and even splendor that it did under Solomon. His reign was remembered in the history of Israel as the Golden Age.

The Bible tells an almost legendary story about Solomon's meeting with the queen of Sheba. Sheba was an ancient country that was probably situated in the southwestern part of the Arabian peninsula. King Solomon's name had become known there because of the expeditions he sent out across the Red Sea. The queen of Sheba, hearing about both the magnificence and the wisdom of the king of Israel, decided to visit him. She arrived in Jerusalem at the head of a camel caravan loaded with perfumes, gold, and precious stones.

Solomon welcomed the queen with great pomp and ceremony. He arranged for her to travel about his kingdom; she was very impressed by the splendid building projects he showed to her, especially by the exceptionally beautiful Temple. She also admired the way that Solomon had organized his government; she took an interest in every detail of it.

After she had seen and admired everything, she began to test the intelligence of Solomon, about which she had heard so much. She asked questions and riddles of Solomon on a number of subjects, and King Solomon was able to answer everything. In the end, the queen had to admit she couldn't outwit him. She declared,

"The report was true which I heard in my own land of your affairs and of your wisdom, but I did not believe the reports until I came and my own eyes had seen it; and behold, the half was not told me; your wisdom and prosperity surpass the report which I heard. Happy are your wives! Happy are these your servants who continually stand before you and hear your wisdom! Blessed be the Lord your God, who has delighted in you and set you on the throne of Israel."

(1 Kings 10:6-9)

At that point, the king of Israel and the queen of Sheba exchanged gifts. The queen gave him gold and precious stones; for his gift to her, he told her to choose what she most desired. Finally, the queen of Sheba returned again to her own country, convinced that Solomon and his kingdom enjoyed a special love and protection from God.

7 Solomon took many wives,
some from foreign nations.
Some of them influenced him
to allow worship of the gods
of their countries.
Many Israelites forgot
their special relationship
to the one true God.
A prophet of God foretold
the division of the kingdom
by tearing his cloak
into twelve parts,
representing the twelve tribes.

In Solomon's time, the greatness and wealth of a monarch were measured by the number of wives he had. Each king possessed a harem in which his women lived; he was considered the husband and lord of all of them, even if he loved only one queen in a special way. These marriage customs were deeply rooted in the culture of the times, and only much later did they change.

Solomon too had many wives. He took some of these wives in order to establish a family relationship with one or another of the rulers of the neighboring kingdoms. Tradition says that Solomon had a thousand wives. Such an exaggerated, large number, however, was really intended just to give a sense of Solomon's wealth and magnificence.

Solomon's foreign wives contributed to the religious decline both of the king and of his kingdom. Many of his wives worshiped idols. They were attached to their pagan cults, and they each wanted their own temples, their own priests, and their own religious practices. Solomon allowed them all of this; and through their influence, the Israelite people began to get their own religious ideas and practices mixed up. They gave up their faith in the one true God and in the commandments of the Law that he had delivered to them. When Solomon grew older, he himself was tempted by this false worship, in spite of all his wisdom; and he ended by erecting altars and sanctuaries for various idols.

God became angry because Solomon had forgotten all God's promises and had turned away from God. God said to Solomon,

"Because you have deliberately broken your covenant with me and disobeyed my commands, I promise that I will take the kingdom away from you and give it to one of your officials. However, for the sake of your father David I will not do this in your lifetime, but during the reign of your son. And I will not take the whole kingdom away from him; instead, I will leave him one tribe for the sake of my servant David and for the sake of Jerusalem, the city I have made my own."

(1 Kings 11:11-13 TEV)

This is exactly what did happen. The official turned out to be Jeroboam, who had once been an officer of Solomon's in charge of forced-labor construction. While in this position, he had caused a revolt of the laborers and then had had to flee into exile in Egypt in order to avoid arrest. He was in Egypt when Solomon died.

The Hebrew prophet Ahijah prophesied that Jeroboam would one day be king of Israel, following a split between the southern and northern parts of the country. The prophet tore his mantle, or cloak, into twelve parts, symbolizing the twelve tribes of Israel; he gave ten of the pieces to Jeroboam, showing that Jeroboam would one day rule over the ten northern tribes.

8 When Solomon died,
his kingdom split in two.
The northern ten tribes
rebelled against the taxes
and forced labor
of Rehoboam, Solomon's son.
Jeroboam became ruler
of this kingdom, called Israel.
Jeroboam placed golden calves
at two centers of worship.
The southern kingdom, Judah,
remained loyal to Rehoboam.

Solomon died in 931 B.C. His son Rehoboam immediately was made king by the tribe of Judah. Then Rehoboam traveled to the ancient city of Shechem in the center of the country, where representatives of the northern tribes were gathered to recognize the new king.

These northern tribes, however, had two serious complaints against the monarchy. One was the taxes, or tribute of crops and goods, which these tribes had to pay the royal court, while the tribe of Judah was exempt from these taxes. Their other complaint concerned the forced labor these tribes had to provide for the monarchy.

So at Shechem Rehoboam found himself standing in front of a people unwilling to accept him automatically; they wanted to set some conditions. They said to Rehoboam,

"Your father made our yoke heavy. Now therefore lighten the hard service of your father and his heavy yoke upon us, and we will serve you."
(1 Kings 12:4)

Rehoboam told them he would give them his reply after three days, and, meanwhile, he sought the advice of the men of his court. These advisers, who had gained a great deal of experience with Solomon, told him,

"If you will be a servant to this people today and serve them, and speak good words to them when you answer them, then they will be your servants for ever." (1 Kings 12:7)

However, Rehoboam was not satisfied with this advice. He decided to consult the young men who had grown up with him at the royal court and who were preparing to become his ministers. The young men advised him to be strict and severe, and this was the advice that he took. On the third day, the king appeared before the assembly at Shechem with a harsh expression on his face.and gave his reply,

"My father placed heavy burdens on you; I will make them even heavier. He beat you with whips; I'll flog you with bullwhips!"
(1 Kings 12:14 TEV)

The crowd protested loudly, shouting,

"Down with David and his family! What have they ever done for us? Men of Israel, let's go home! Let Rehoboam look out for himself!"
(1 Kings 12:16 TEV)

To calm the people, Rehoboam sent Adoniram, who was in charge of forced labor. The angry people stoned him to death. Alarmed, King Rehoboam mounted his chariot and fled back to Jerusalem.

Jeroboam, back from exile in Egypt, took charge of organizing the ten rebellious tribes. They proclaimed him king at Shechem. In order to break all remaining ties with Jerusalem and to eliminate any religious reasons for going down to the Temple in Jerusalem, Jeroboam had two sanctuaries erected in the north. One was at Bethel, the site of Jacob's dream, and the other at Dan, in the extreme north of the country. He ordered a golden calf placed in each of these sanctuaries, and said to the people, "Behold your gods, O Israel, who brought you up out of the land of Egypt" (1 Kings 12:28).

What Jeroboam did was definitely against the divine commandments; it promoted idolatry. And the division between the northern and southern tribes became a religious split as well as a political split.

The two tribes of Judah and Benjamin remained loyal to Rehoboam. He wanted to make war on Israel, but the prophet Shemaiah advised him against it. For the moment, there was no war between the two kingdoms: the southern kingdom, called Judah, and the northern kingdom, which took for itself the name Israel.

Kingdom of Israel

Shechem

Bethel

Jordan River

Jerusalem

Dead Sea

Kingdom of Judah

9 The ark of the covenant was
the center of Judah's worship.
The golden calf became
the center of Israel's worship,
although God's law forbids
making images of God.
God promised punishment:
the death of Jeroboam's son
and continued rebellion.

Jeroboam had not intended to change gods when he built two sanctuaries and placed golden calves inside them; he had intended to remain faithful to Yahweh, the God of the Hebrews. But he thought he had to distinguish worship in the northern kingdom from that in Jerusalem. The Temple in Jerusalem possessed the ark of the covenant, so he chose another symbol of divinity—the one used by the Canaanite peoples to represent their god, Baal. Baal was represented by the figure of a young bull, standing for the power and fruitfulness of God, who had given life to human beings and to other parts of nature.

By choosing such a symbol, however, Jeroboam ran the risk of confusing his people about who God was and about how God was to be worshiped. He broke God's law, which forbids the fashioning of any image of God.

One day Jeroboam was offering a sacrifice on one of the very altars that he had ordered erected. A prophet of God approached and hurled a curse at the altar. The altar split in two, and the ashes that had been spread out on it were scattered to the four winds. When Jeroboam raised his hand as a signal for his men to seize the prophet, the king's hand was immediately paralyzed. Frightened, the rebel king then implored the prophet to cure his paralysis. The prophet did so, but then refused to accept any reward for it. He said to Jeroboam, "If you give me half your house, I will not go in with you. And I will not eat bread or drink water in this place" (1 Kings 13:8).

God's punishment was not slow in coming. Jeroboam's son suddenly became very ill, greatly alarming the household of the king. So Jeroboam sent his wife, dressed up as a woman of the people, to the prophet Ahijah. Ahijah was the prophet who had once predicted that Jeroboam would be king. Jeroboam's wife was to ask for the miracle of a cure for their son.

The prophet recognized immediately that it was the king's wife who had come to him. He said to her to go tell Jeroboam,

"I chose you from among the people and made you ruler of my people Israel. I took the kingdom away from David's descendants and gave it to you. But you have not been like my servant David. . . . You have committed far greater sins than those who ruled before you. You have rejected me and have aroused my anger by making idols and metal images to worship. . . . Because of this I will bring disaster on your dynasty and will kill all your male descendants." (1 Kings 14:7-10 TEV)

In this way God announced that the kingdom of Israel would be continually tormented by internal struggles and that the throne would be in constant danger of takeover by others.

The author of these Bible stories interpreted human disasters to the king and his family as God's punishment on the king because he had disobeyed God's law. Frequently these punishments served to make the king aware of the seriousness of his sin. In the mind of the writer, no ruler could disobey God by commiting idolatry and expect to go unpunished.

10 Egypt attacked Judah
and plundered the Temple
and palace in Jerusalem.
The prophet Shemaiah
said that this was punishment
for idolatry under Rehoboam.

The southern kingdom that Rehoboam ruled over was called the kingdom of Judah. Its capital continued to be the beautiful city of Jerusalem. Judah was smaller than Jeroboam's northern kingdom of Israel, but it had the advantage of being much more compact and therefore easier to govern. And its geographic position and natural features made it easier to defend.

Even though Judah possessed the unique Temple in Jerusalem, the southern kingdom, just like the northern kingdom, allowed pagan religious cults. Sanctuaries for these prohibited cults were built, and even King Rehoboam was guilty of idol worship.

A terrible misfortune fell on Judah. Rehoboam had not reigned for five years before the Egyptian pharaoh Shishak attacked him. The pharaoh invaded Judah with 1,200 chariots and 60,000 horses. One by one they overcame the fortresses strategically spread along Judah's borders and then they made their way all the way to Jerusalem. The treasures of both the Temple and the royal palace were plundered. The two hundred golden shields with which Solomon had decorated his palace were carried off. Even the northern kingdom was partially invaded by the Egyptians.

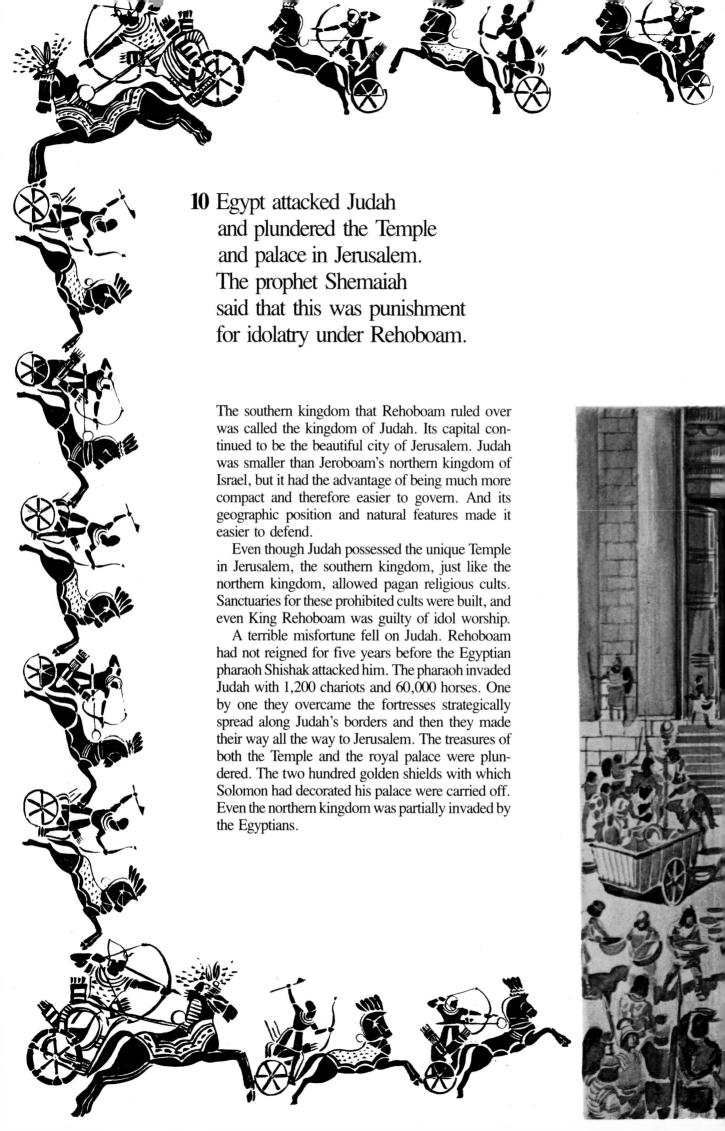

The meaning of this terrible misfortune was interpreted by the prophet Shemaiah. He explained that God had abandoned Rehoboam and allowed him to fall into the hands of Shishak because Rehoboam first had abandoned God.

Touched by the grace of God, both the king and elders of Israel recognized their error and knew that they deserved a just punishment. The prophet Shemaiah explained to them that because of this, God would not permit Jerusalem to be totally destroyed. However, God intended to leave them subject to the pharaoh. "In that way," the Lord said, "they will learn the difference between serving me and serving earthly rulers."

God's words reminded the king that obedience to God will bring happiness and disobedience to God can result in slavery to earthly rulers.

Although Judah did enjoy some happy years, relations between Judah and Israel were always tense and threatening. The split between them grew greater and greater—and it was to be permanent.

As for Rehoboam, the biblical writer judged him quite severely when he wrote that Rehoboam "reigned seventeen years in Jerusalem. . . . And he did evil, for he did not set his heart to seek the Lord" (2 Chronicles 12:13-14).

Elah

Zimri   Tibni   Omri   Ahab   Ahaziah   Joram

Baasha

Nadab

Jeroboam

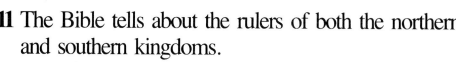

11 The Bible tells about the rulers of both the northern and southern kingdoms.

Its main concern is whether the kings and people were faithful to their covenant with God.

Two books in the Bible—1 Kings and 2 Kings—present a history of the two Israelite kingdoms. The accounts of some events are brief and sketchy; others are told in more detail.

This chronicle of the kingdoms tells about times of stability and even of splendor—for example, Israel in the time of Omri, and Judah in the times of Hezekiah and Josiah. However, the author is concerned most about making a religious judgment on each of the two kingdoms and, especially, on each of the kings. Have the kingdom and the king resisted idolatry and remained faithful to the Lord?

The two books of Kings show a clear distinction between the two kingdoms. On the one hand, the kingdom of Judah, centered around worship in the Temple and always ruled over by a king descended from David, is seen as basically faithful to the covenant of the Chosen People with their God. The throne of Judah passed regularly from father to son, in fulfillment of God's promise to David that his descendants would always sit upon the throne.

The kingdom of Israel, however, is seen from its beginning as straying from the covenant, starting with ''the sin of Jeroboam,'' representing God by the image of a golden calf. As a result of this sin, Israel experienced continual political unrest. Even in fairly peaceful times, the governments of Israel were overthrown one after another, and the kings and their families were put to death. In two hundred years, there were nineteen kings—eight of whom died violently—and nine revolts. In Judah, during the same period, there were only eleven kings, all in the line of David.

While the overall judgment of the books of Kings clearly favors the kingdom of Judah, the judgment on individual religious behavior is quite impartial: The behavior of nearly every king is condemned. The author of the books of Kings is sometimes called ''the Deuteronomist.'' This is because the author always judges the fact of history according to the basic principle, or idea, in Deuteronomy: The people of Israel, and, in particular, their kings, will enjoy prosperity only if they remain faithful to the covenant with God; otherwise they will be condemned to trouble within the kingdom and invasions by their enemies. If the king is the one who first betrays the covenant, then he is responsible for the ruin of the nation.

Rehoboam

Abijam

Asa

Jehoram   Ahaziah   Athaliah   Joash   Amaziah   Uzzia

Jehoshaphat

Menahem

hu   Jehoahaz   Jehoash   Jeroboam II   Zechariah   Shallum

Pekahiah

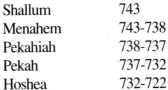

Pekah

Jeroboam	931-910 BC		Jehoahaz (Joahaz)	814-798
Nadab	910-909		Jehoash (Joash)	798-783
Baasha	909-886		Jeroboam II	783-743
Elah	886-885		Zechariah	743
Zimri	885		Shallum	743
Tibni			Menahem	743-738
Omri	885-874		Pekahiah	738-737
Ahab	874-853		Pekah	737-732
Ahaziah	853-852		Hoshea	732-722
Joram (Jehoram)	852-841		Deportation	
Jehu	841-814		to Assyria	722

Hoshea

Kings of Israel

Kings of Judah

Zedekiah

Rehoboam	931-913 BC		Ahaz	736-716
Abijam	913-911		Hezekiah	716-687
Asa	911-870		Manasseh	687-642
Jehoshaphat	870-848		Amon	642-640
Jehoram	848-841		Josiah	640-609
Ahaziah	841		Jehoahaz	609
Athaliah	841-835		Jehoiakim	609-598
Joash (Jehoash)	835-796		Jehoiachin	598-597
Amaziah	796-781		Zedekiah	597-587
Uzziah (Azariah)	781-740		Babylonian Exile	587
Jotham	740-736			

Jehoiachin

Jehoiakim

ham   Ahaz   Hezekiah   Manasseh   Amon   Josiah

Jehoahaz

12 In Judah, Rehoboam's grandson,
King Asa, tried to end
the worship of idols.
But in Israel Baasha,
who became king by killing
the entire royal family,
favored idol worship.
Israel and Judah both sought
the friendship of the king
of Syria.

In the kingdom of Judah, Rehoboam's favorite son, Abijah, succeeded his father. He fought against Jeroboam and won an important victory, which enabled the Judeans to occupy the southern hills of Ephraim. The victory was considered a sign of God's approval because Jerusalem had remained faithful to the true worship of Yahweh.

But Abijah reigned for only three years; then his son Asa succeeded him on the throne. Asa was a good king, and he had a long reign of almost forty years. One of his most important accomplishments was his effort to purify the "Yahwist" religion—the true religion of the Chosen People—from the pagan additions and contaminations that had crept into it over the years. In carrying out this religious task, Asa even went against his own grandmother, who worshiped idols; he removed her from the position of being queen-mother. In spite of his efforts, Asa was only partially successful in ridding Judah of pagan influences.

Asa continued fighting with Israel; he helped to bring Jeroboam to ruin. Then Asa had to face a danger that threatened from the south. A throng of nomads from Ethiopia invaded, destroying everything in their path. Asa met them in battle, defeated them, and pushed them back towards the south; then he returned to Jerusalem loaded down with war booty.

Asa won great fame and respect through this victory over the Ethiopians; this enabled him to dedicate himself more completely to his favorite project: religious reform. He was urged on in this work by the prophet Azariah, who declared that the covenant with the Lord needed to be renewed by the people. This was done. Once again, the people began to seek after the Lord, the God of their fathers and mothers.

By now, the ruler in the northern kingdom of Israel was Baasha. He was not the son of Jeroboam. He was the leader of a group that had rebelled and exterminated the entire royal family. Baasha then had had himself crowned king. He too reigned for a long time, nearly twenty-four years. During his reign he favored idol worship, as Jeroboam had, partly to keep his people religiously separated from Jerusalem. Baasha too experienced the threats of a prophet who announced God's punishment. The prophet Jehu brought this message from God for Baasha:

"You were a nobody, but I made you the leader of my people Israel. And now you have sinned like Jeroboam and have led my people into sin. Their sins have aroused my anger." (1 Kings 16:2 TEV)

Baasha formed a political alliance (people joined together for a common purpose) with Ben-hadad I, the Aramean (Syrian) king of Damascus, so that he could invade Judah without any threat from the Arameans. What Baasha did not know was that Asa had given Ben-hadad gifts of silver and gold, convincing him to switch sides. Suddenly Baasha found himself invaded from Damascus when he least expected it—by his own one-time ally. Israel lost some important territory in the north to Ben-hadad and also had to give up its attack on Judah.

Asa gained a period of peace for Judah by dealing with Ben-hadad, but going to the king of Syria for help was a mistake. The prophet Hanani scolded Asa severely for this, even though he was otherwise a good king.

"You relied on the king of Syria, and did not rely on the Lord your God. . . . You have done foolishly; . . . from now on you will have wars."
(2 Chronicles 16:7, 9)

In the last years of his life, Asa was cruel to some of his own people. He became ill and died without really turning back to the Lord. His body was prepared for burial with spices and perfumed oils and then buried in the tomb which he had carved out for himself in the city of David.

13 Israel continued to be
a land of rebellions.
Zimri tried to be king
but died in the flames
of his own palace.
Omri became a strong king
and made Samaria
the new capital city.
Though a brave ruler,
he worshiped idols.

Baasha's son Elah reigned briefly in Israel. Then Zimri, an army officer who led a division of chariots, carried out a plot against the throne. He killed Elah during a banquet, and went on to destroy all of Baasha's family, just as the prophet Jehu had predicted. However, Zimri succeeded in reigning for only seven days because the army refused to recognize him. Instead, the army proclaimed as king its commander-in-chief, Omri. Omri besieged the city of Tirzah, which was then Israel's capital. Within its walls Zimri had taken refuge; he barricaded himself in the royal palace, and, when all hope of victory was lost, he set the palace on fire and died in the flames.

After a brief struggle with Tibni, Omri became king. His family became Israel's first ruling dynasty, which continued for nearly a half century. There were other attempted rebellions in the first few years, but Omri successfully put them down.

Once Omri established a stable government, he decided to build a new capital to replace Tirzah, damaged by many wars. With six thousand pieces of

silver, he purchased a steep-sided hill located almost in the center of the kingdom, along the main north-south road. There he built Samaria, a splendid, strong new capital city. Omri's choice of a site was excellent; for a century and a half, no enemy was able to conquer it.

Omri seems to have been a particularly brave and competent ruler. His reign was important enough for the kingdom of Israel to be described in documents of surrounding countries as "the house of Omri." Another sign of his great reputation was the fact that he was able to arrange for his son Ahab to marry Jezebel, daughter of a Phoenician king.

Omri took part in frequent frontier wars with the Arameans of Damascus, but he was on good terms with the kingdom of Judah. The almost constant border wars between Israel and Judah stopped. This was partly because Omri needed to be free for the struggle with Damascus (Syria).

Omri did not do so well in his religious practices, however. He obviously worshiped idols, for the Bible remarks of him that he "did what was evil in the sight of the Lord, and did more evil than all who were before him" (1 Kings 16:25). Always the Bible writer makes a judgment in regard to the king's attitude towards the "Yahwist" religion, the worship of the one true God. If a king favored idol worship, he was judged to be evil, because such a king interfered with God's plan for his Chosen People.

The most important historical event of Omri's era was the rebirth of Assyrian power. Omri's reign occurred at the same time as King Ashurnasirpal's reign in Assyria. This king began a period of expansion for Assyria and forced the little kingdoms around him to pay him tribute. Soon both Israel and Judah would have a very powerful Assyria to deal with.

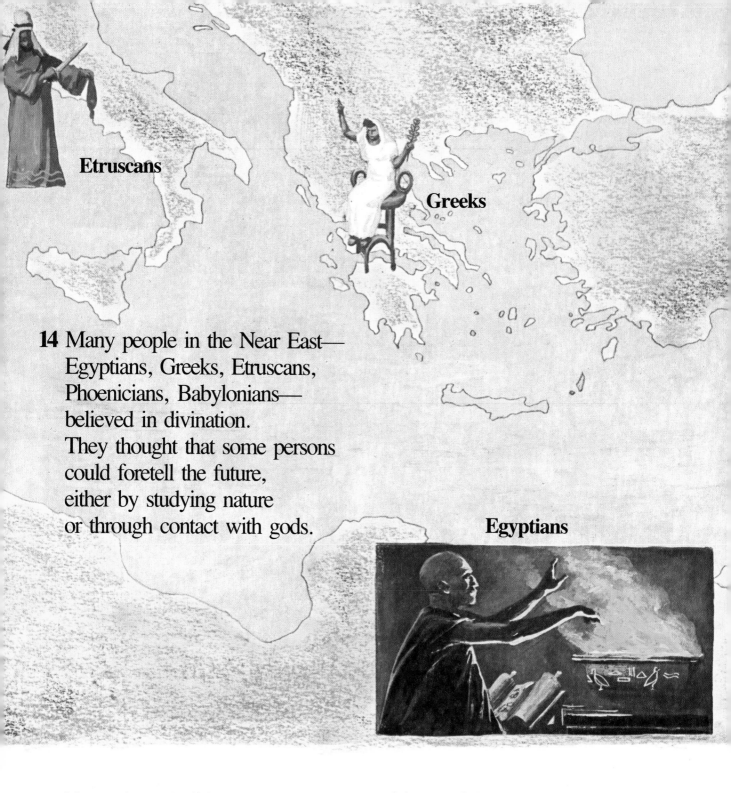

Etruscans

Greeks

14 Many people in the Near East—
Egyptians, Greeks, Etruscans,
Phoenicians, Babylonians—
believed in divination.
They thought that some persons
could foretell the future,
either by studying nature
or through contact with gods.

Egyptians

Many ancient and primitive peoples believed that particular individuals were able to understand hidden mysteries and predict future happenings. The civilizations of the ancient Near East and Greece, especially, had persons with these special powers. Some of them had the duty of divining, or predicting, future events of interest either to the public authorities or to private persons. These diviners shared only some characteristics with the "prophets," who were spiritual guides in ancient Israel and Judah; so they were commonly called by names other than "prophet." Often they were called "divines," and their art was called "divination" and not "prophecy."

There were two main types of divination: "inductive" divination and divination by intuition. Inductive divination was carried out according to certain established rules or patterns, for example, by exam-

ining natural phenomena such as the flights of birds or the patterns of lightning bolts. In intuitive divination, however, some direct contact was made with a supernatural force; this contact was usually established through a dreamlike state or a state of ecstasy. In addition to these kinds of divination, there were attempts to communicate with the souls of the dead. This practice, called "necromancy," corresponds with modern-day "spiritualism."

Among the ancient Egyptians, divines were peaceful officials serving in the temples; they were called "scribes of the divine book." From their books, they attempted to learn favorable times for sacred ceremonies and to provide the words to accompany these ceremonies. They also functioned as healers and magicians. The magicians attempted to influence these supernatural forces for their own purposes. What the magician tried to do could be

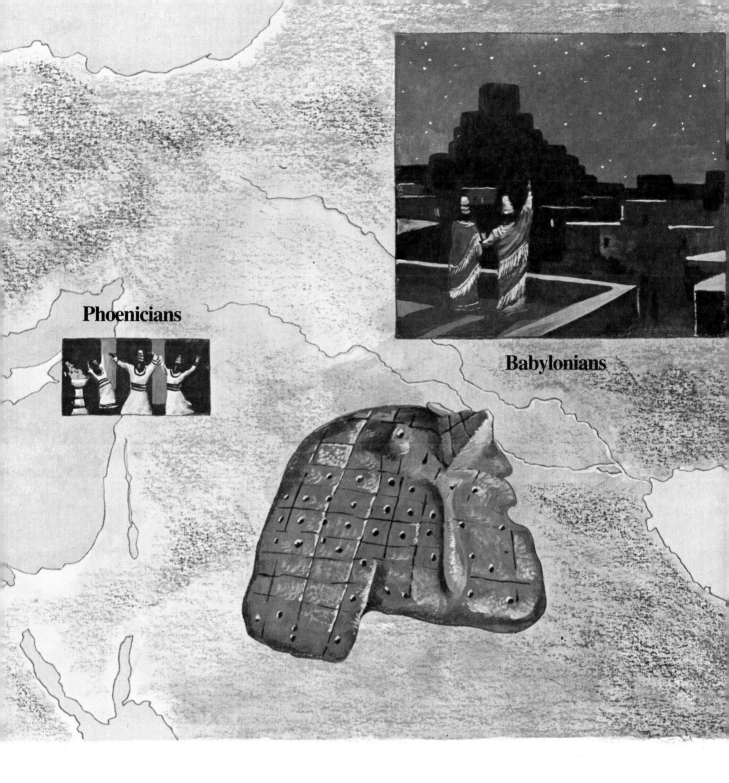

Phoenicians

Babylonians

good (healing or liberating someone) or for evil (harming or working black magic on someone).

In Babylonia, the divines were called "seers," and they studied the various positions of the stars and planets as the key to understanding. (This study is called astrology.) They also attempted to obtain knowledge from the examination of the entrails, or insides, of animals; they thought certain areas of entrails corresponded to various zones of the stars. These practices spread from Asia Minor into Italy, where the Etruscans had "soothsayers" who claimed to learn the divine will by examining the entrails of animals. In Babylonia, also, divination tended to blend into magic.

In ancient Rome, the soothsayers were called "augurs." They practiced divination by examining the flights of birds and other events in nature in order to discover good or bad omens.

Intuitive divination was found among the ancient Phoenicians, who practiced what was called "ecstatic prophetism." Stimulated by the music of the harp, the divine was overcome with convulsive dance movements; in a state of ecstasy he lost the sense of the world around him and spoke words that were thought to come from the gods. In ancient Greece, this same practice was found in the Temple of Apollo at Delphi, where the priestess, Pythia, delivered the oracles, or messages, thought to come from the pagan god Apollo.

15 Among the Hebrews, prophets
spoke in God's name
and with God's authority.
They reminded people of
their covenant with God.

Among the Israelites all types of divination were
strictly forbidden, as was using magic or consulting
the gods of other people.

"There shall not be found among you . . . any
one who practices divination, a soothsayer, or an
augur, or a sorcerer, or a charmer, or a medium, or
a wizard, or a necromancer. For whoever does
these things is an abomination to the Lord."

(Deuteronomy 18:10-12)

The people of God were supposed to rely only on
the Lord God. In time God raised up prophets who
spoke in his name, who made known his will to the
people, and, when necessary, announced some
future events. While foretelling the future was certainly a part of the job God gave the prophets, it was
not the most important part. In the Bible, the word
prophet, from the Greek, corresponds to the Hebrew
word *nabi*. It means someone who speaks in the
name of God and with God's authority, someone
who corrects, someone who warns by foretelling
judgments and misfortunes to come, and who con-
soles by announcing God's future salvation.

Unique among all the prophets of the Israelites
was Moses. Moses was the spokesperson between
God and the people in the extraordinary events of the
exodus out of Egypt and in the establishment of the
covenant with the one true God.

The Hebrew prophets who came after Moses
were above all the defenders of the covenant. If they
interfered in the affairs of the Hebrew kingdoms, as
they often did, it was to keep the people aware of
their special relationship with God. When Samuel
established the Hebrew monarchy and chose as king
first Saul and then David, he acted in the name of
God. Nathan was doing the same when he foretold
the future of the dynasty of David, openly pointed
out the sins of the king, and intervened to make sure
Solomon succeeded David on the throne; in all this,
he too acted in the name of God.

The prophets worked and spoke in order to keep
the people and kings faithful to the true religion and
to the covenant. Some prophets did not leave any
writings behind them (at least that we know of).

Examples are Samuel; Nathan; Ahijah, who warned Jeroboam that his children would not follow him on the throne; and, finally, the great figures of Elijah and Elisha.

There were other prophets whose words and preaching were written down, often in verse, either by themselves or by their disciples; these writings have come down to us as some of the books of the Bible. The first of these great prophets were Amos and Hosea, who preached in the eighth century B.C. in the northern kingdom of Israel. A little later, in the same century, Isaiah and Micah were active in the southern kingdom of Judah. Jeremiah and Ezekiel preached around the time of the end of the kingdom of Judah in 587 B.C. and the beginning of the Babylonian exile. Haggai and Zechariah were prophets after the exile, when the Israelites were back in their own land.

Each prophet received a "call," or "vocation," from God. God's call manifested itself in mysterious ways, but there was never any doubt that there was a call. From that time on, the prophet was a channel for the "word of God," which the prophet delivered publicly after the message first came to him inwardly. Sometimes the prophets had visions.

The prophet dedicated his life totally to his mission. Often his mission caused the prophet to oppose the reigning kings, the levitical priests, any false prophets, or the people at large, who so often tended towards superstition, idolatry, and oppression. The Hebrew prophets called people back to the worship of God and defended the rights of the poor against social injustices and abuses of power by rulers and officials.

16 During the reign of King Ahab
and his wife Jezebel,
Elijah the prophet challenged
the idolatrous worship of Baal.
The Bible tells about many miracles.
He brought a widow's son
back to life, and
he kept her kitchen
supplied with flour and oil.

King Omri of Israel was succeeded by his son Ahab, a king famous for the buildings which he had constructed to beautify his capital, Samaria, as well as the cities of Megiddo and Jericho. Ahab was also noted for his organizing ability in both politics and trade.

The religious practices of the king and his people, however, went from bad to worse. The trouble began when Ahab took as his wife Jezebel, the daughter of the king of Sidon in Phoenicia. The strong-willed new queen not only demanded the construction in Samaria of a temple to Baal, her pagan god, but she also urged the people to take part in worship practices that were both idolatrous and cruel. She persecuted the followers of the true religion of the Israelites. Ahab did nothing to stop any of this.

Resistance to these practices came from one of the greatest biblical prophets: Elijah. His first act was quite dramatic. He went directly to Ahab in his palace to announce God's punishment. Elijah told Ahab,

"As the Lord, the God of Israel lives, before
whom I stand, there shall be neither dew nor rain
these years except by my word." (1 Kings 17:1)

Elijah then had to flee from the persecution of the angry king. He took refuge by a brook called Cherith. Here, the Bible says, he was fed by ravens, who

brought bread and meat to him both morning and evening. Meanwhile, just as Elijah had prophesied, rain ceased entirely and everything began to dry up. Finally not even the brook had any more water. Drought and famine were everywhere.

Elijah slowly made his way to Zarephath, a city near Sidon in Phoenicia. At the entrance to the city he came upon a woman gathering wood. He called this woman to himself and said, "Give me some water to drink." Then he also asked for something to eat. The woman replied,

"By the living Lord your God I swear that I don't have any bread. All I have is a handful of flour in a bowl and a bit of olive oil in a jar. I came here to gather some firewood to take back home and prepare what little I have for my son and me. That will be our last meal, and then we will starve to death."

"Don't worry," Elijah said to her. "Go on and prepare your meal. But first make a small loaf from what you have and bring it to me, and then prepare the rest for you and your son. For this is what the Lord, the God of Israel, says: 'The bowl will not run out of flour or the jar run out of oil before the day that I, the Lord, send rain.' "

(1 Kings 17:12-14 TEV)

It happened as Elijah had said. Elijah, the woman, and her child all ate, and the flour and oil were continually replenished. Elijah continued to be a guest in the house.

One day the child suddenly became ill and died shortly thereafter. Elijah took the dead body of the child to the upper chamber and laid the body out on the bed. Then Elijah prayed to God. He stretched himself out on the child three times as if he were trying to transfer his own breath to the child. Then he cried to the Lord, "O Lord my God, let this child's soul come into him again" (1 Kings 17:21).

The Lord heard the cry of Elijah. The child returned to life. Elijah gave him back to his mother with the remark, "See, your son lives."

The woman said to Elijah, "Now I know that you are a man of God, and that the word of the Lord in your mouth is truth" (1 Kings 17:24).

17 Elijah fled from Ahab
because the king blamed
a drought on Elijah.
Later Elijah returned
and called for a contest
between Baal, Ahab's god,
and the God of Elijah.

Since the time that Elijah had first faced King Ahab to announce that there would be drought throughout the kingdom, the two had not seen each other. The king had had searches conducted everywhere without finding Elijah. Meanwhile Queen Jezebel persecuted the worshipers of Yahweh and had them killed. At the same time, she protected the prophets of Baal and Asherah. The prophets of these false gods were numerous: 450 prophets of Baal and about 400 for Asherah.

One day Ahab called in the steward over his household, Obadiah. Obadiah was a good man. He had hidden more than a hundred prophets of Yahweh in caves near Samaria to protect them from Jezebel's anger and to feed them secretly. As Ahab and Obadiah stood on the terrace of the royal palace looking out over the city of Samaria devastated by the drought and famine, Ahab told Obadiah,

"Go through the land . . . to all the valleys; perhaps we may find grass and save the horses and mules alive, and not lose some of the animals." (1 Kings 18:5)

They divided the kingdom in two, and each went to search one part of it. As Obadiah went on his way, he met Elijah. As soon as he recognized him, the steward got down from his chariot and fell down on his face before him. The prophet told Obadiah to go back and inform Ahab that Elijah had returned to Israel.

Obadiah was terrified at the idea of such a thing; he would be in serious trouble with the king if Elijah vanished again. Obadiah explained how he had saved many servants of Yahweh, and he begged to be excused from going back to Ahab with this message. Elijah reassured Obadiah that he would not disappear, and followed Obadiah back to the palace.

As soon as Ahab saw Elijah he called to him, "Is it you, you troubler of Israel?" And he answered, "I have not troubled Israel; but you have, and your father's house, because you have forsaken the commandments of the Lord and followed the Baals." (1 Kings 18:17-18)

At that point Elijah challenged Ahab: to a test of strength between Jezebel's god and Elijah's God. Ahab should send to Mount Carmel all 450 of the prophets of Baal and all 400 of those of Asherah. Alone Elijah would meet them and would demonstrate which god was the true God of Israel.

Although Ahab had earlier threatened Elijah with death, he was tired; he was also concerned about the terrible famine that was destroying his kingdom and his people. He was very aware, too, that Elijah was a powerful prophet. After all, with a single word Elijah had closed up the sky, and from that time on not a single drop of water had fallen on the land.

And so Ahab decided to accept Elijah's challenge. He spread throughout the kingdom the news that Elijah would meet the prophets of Baal and Asherah on Mount Carmel. It would be decided once and for all which was the true God, worthy of the Israelites' worship. Ahab sent out a proclamation summoning all citizens to Mount Carmel.

18 On Mount Carmel
Elijah stood alone
against the prophets of Baal.
He mocked their efforts
and their god.
Then God answered Elijah's
prayer and sent fire
to consume his offering.

On top of Mount Carmel all the prophets of Baal stood together. Elijah, alone, stood off by himself. The people were all gathered around. Elijah approached the people and said,

> "How much longer will it take you to make up your minds? If the Lord is God, worship him; but if Baal is God, worship him!"

(1 Kings 18:21 TEV)

Then the prophet of Yahweh issued his challenge. The prophets of Baal were to prepare a young bull to offer to their god; they were to slaughter the animal and lay it out on a pile of wood, but without setting fire to the wood. Elijah would do the same. He said,

> "Then let the prophets of Baal pray to their god, and I will pray to the Lord, and the god who answers by sending fire—he is God."

(1 Kings 18:24 TEV)

The people agreed that this was a fair test, and they stood around awaiting the result.

The prophets of Baal began. They took a young bull, slaughtered it, and laid it out on a pile of wood. Then they began to call out the name of their god with loud cries and fervent prayers. They called on the name of Baal from morning until noon, pleading, "Answer us, Baal!" But nothing happened; there was no answer. Elijah mocked them, saying,

> "Pray louder! He is a god! Maybe he is daydreaming or relieving himself, or perhaps he's gone off on a trip! Or maybe he's sleeping, and you've got to wake him up!"

(1 Kings 18:27 TEV)

The prophets of Baal grew more and more frantic. They danced their sacred dances. Some of them slashed themselves, which was one of the customs of their worship, and then covered themselves with blood. But the young bull lay untouched where it had been placed. No fire came.

Then Elijah came forward. He drew the people around. He took twelve stones, symbolizing the twelve tribes of Israel, and constructed an altar with them. He dug a trench around the altar. He piled up the wood and placed a young bull on top of it. Then he said, "Fill four jars with water and pour it on the offering and the wood" (1 Kings 18:33 TEV).

It was done. Elijah asked that water be poured on the wood again. And yet again. The animal and the wood were thoroughly soaked, and the water ran down into the trench around the altar. Then, at the time for the sacrifice, Elijah the prophet came forward and said,

"O Lord, the God of Abraham, Isaac, and Jacob, prove now that you are the God of Israel and that I am your servant and have done all this at your command. Answer me, Lord, answer me, so that this people will know that you, the Lord, are God and that you are bringing them back to yourself."

(1 Kings 18:36-37 TEV)

A fire came down from heaven that consumed the burnt offering, the wood, the twelve stones, and the water that had filled up the trench. At this sight all the people fell down on their faces and cried, "The Lord is God! The Lord alone is God!"

The prophets of Baal were executed. Shortly afterwards, the sky covered with dark clouds, the wind blew, and the long-awaited rain began to fall in torrents.

did not last long.
Threatened by Queen Jezebel
with death,
and tired of serving God,
Elijah fled
to the holy mountain Sinai.
He expected God to speak
to him with power and violence.
Instead, God came in
a still, small voice.

lived. Queen Jezebel was furious and vowed to kill Elijah. Once more, Elijah had to flee. He headed south into the hot, dry desert, traveling as far as he could. There he collapsed, prostrate, tired of persecution and of flight. He wanted to die: "It is enough; now, O Lord, take away my life; for I am no better than my father" (1 Kings 19:4).

Elijah fell asleep desiring simply to give up. He was awakened by an angel of the Lord, who gave him fresh water and a cake of bread to eat. Then the angel commanded him to go on, warning him that the journey was far from over. He was to travel all the way to Mount Sinai, the very mountain on which God had established the covenant with the Chosen People. When he reached the holy mountain, he was to wait for God to show himself.

And there he came to a cave, and lodged there; and behold the word of the Lord came to him, and he said to him, "What are you doing here, Elijah?" He said, "I have been very jealous for the

Lord, the God of hosts: for the people of Israel have forsaken thy covenant, thrown down thy altars, and slain thy prophets with the sword; and I, even I only, am left; and they seek my life, to take it away.'' And he said, ''Go forth, and stand upon the mount before the Lord.'' And behold, the Lord passed by, and a great and strong wind rent the mountains, and broke in pieces the rocks before the Lord, but the Lord was not in the wind; and after the wind an earthquake, but the Lord was not in the earthquake; and after the earthquake a fire, but the Lord was not in the fire; and after fire a still, small voice. And when Elijah heard it, he wrapped his face in his mantle and went out and stood at the entrance of the cave.

(1 Kings 19:9-13)

Elijah, in his zeal to defend the covenant and the Law of God, had become impatient and proud. He had decided that a terrible and decisive intervention on the part of God had become necessary. Mighty acts were called for. However, God showed himself not in the majestic and terrible events which Elijah had come to expect—violent wind, earthquake, fire. Instead, God showed himself and spoke to Elijah in the still, small voice of the wind, suggesting the freedom and gentleness of God.

Elijah needed to understand that God's actions do not necessarily take the form that human beings want or expect them to; God manages history in ways which do not always seem appropriate to human judgment.

At the end of this experience, God told Elijah to return to Israel to continue his work and to look for a man named Elisha, who would be his successor.

20 Ahab and Jezebel wanted
Naboth's vineyard,
which was near the palace.
Naboth did not want to sell it.
So the king and queen arranged
for Naboth to be killed.
Elijah confronted Ahab
and announced that
he and Jezebel would both
die violent deaths.

The Bible recounts many stories about the conflict between Ahab, king of Israel, and the prophet Elijah. One of the best known of these stories (which probably occurred before the events of the story told in the last chapter) is the story of Naboth's vineyard.

Naboth owned a large vineyard next to Ahab's winter palace in Jezreel. Ahab decided that he very much wanted the vineyard, and he offered to buy it or give Naboth another one in its place. But Naboth shook his head no. He had inherited this piece of land from his ancestors, and Israel's legal and religious customs said that property must be handed down through the family, unless there were no heirs.

Although the king already had plenty of possessions, he began to pout at Naboth's refusal. He went to his bedchamber and refused to eat. He knew there was no legal way for him to take over the vineyard.

One solution to the problem occurred to Ahab's wife, the evil Jezebel. With incredible wickedness, she wrote a letter in Ahab's name to the elders and leaders of the city; she told them to proclaim a day of fast and penitence as if some great misfortune had befallen the city. Once all the people were assembled, two witnesses were then brought forward who made false statements about Naboth. They accused him of having blasphemed the name of God and cursed the king. These were crimes that called for death, and so Naboth would have to be condemned and executed.

That is exactly what happened. Naboth and his family were taken outside the city and stoned to death. Ahab then was able to take over Naboth's vineyard. Ahab, however, had barely set foot on the property when he was confronted by Elijah. The prophet cried out,

"Have you killed, and also taken possession? . . . Thus says the Lord: 'In the place
where dogs licked up the blood of Naboth shall
dogs lick your own blood.' '' (1 Kings 21:19)

This time Ahab repented of what he had done. He
wept and prayed to God for pardon. For this reason,
the Lord spared him further punishment during his
own life. But the punishment due to Jezebel and to
the house of Ahab was still to come.

21 The Arameans lived
to the north of Israel.
Because Arameans were traders,
people of many lands spoke
their language, Aramaic.
The Aramean kingdom of Syria,
the capital of which was Damascus,
often fought against Israel.

The Aramean people appeared early in the story of the kings, when the Aramean kingdoms of Damascus and Zoba became subject to David and Solomon. When Solomon's kingdom divided after his death, the Aramean kingdom of Damascus became independent. Then, by absorbing some of the small states around it, Aram-Damascus became a dangerous neighbor on Israel's northern border.

Who were the Arameans? Where did they come from? They were the descendants of some Amorite people who had remained nomads living on the edge of the desert west of the Euphrates River, rather than living in cities on the Euphrates. Centuries later, between about the 12th and 11th centuries B.C., they became a distinct people with their own language, Aramaic.

By their continual raids from the desert they gave no end of trouble to the Assyrian people, whose empire centered around the city of Nineveh. Between 1074 B.C. (the death of Tiglath-pileser I of Assyria) and 932 B.C. (the rebirth of Assyrian power with Ashurdan II), the Arameans took advantage of the power vacuum in western Mesopotamia. They established themselves in what would later be called Syria, founding a string of small independent kingdoms: at Aleppo, at Hamath, and at Damascus.

Other groups of Arameans, along with the Chaldeans to whom they were related, moved into central Mesopotamia, settling in the territories extending towards Babylonia and beyond, all the way to the Persian Gulf.

Although they had originally been nomads, the Arameans became skillful merchants and traders. Around the 10th century B.C. they adopted the Phoenician alphabet, and then changed it to make it more suitable as a script for commercial use. Little by little the Aramaic language became a common language and an easy means of communication among various peoples of the Near East. Later, in the 6th century B.C., Aramaic became the official diplomatic language of the Persian Empire.

The Arameans' relationship with Israel was often determined by the rise or fall of Assyrian power. If the Assyrians were occupied fighting against the kingdoms of northern Mesopotamia, then the Aramean kingdoms in Syria usually enjoyed great prosperity (9th century B.C.). The king of Damascus, Ben-hadad I, wished to expand his realm towards the south by attacking the king of Israel, Baasha; he was persuaded to do this, in part, by the king of Judah, Asa. In the course of this struggle, Ben-hadad occupied and devastated the cities of northern Galilee.

Omri, the father of Ahab and the founder of Samaria, could not defeat Ben-hadad I either. He had to yield some cities to him and also allow him the use of Samaria itself as a free trading area. The son of Ben-hadad, even more aggressive than his father, actually besieged Samaria, though he was defeated twice by Ahab.

When Ben-hadad was threatened by the Assyrians and their leader Shalmaneser III, he joined with Ahab's forces in holding off the common enemy. But once the Assyrian danger had passed, he attacked Ahab again. It was in this particular battle that Ahab was killed.

Later, Assyria brought the kingdom of Damascus under its control and successfully put down the continual rebellions which followed. This conquest of Damascus by Assyria gave Israel some rest. Eventually, however, Israel too was to fall to the irresistible power of Assyria.

22 The Syrian king Ben-hadad II
attacked Ahab, king of Judah.
Through careful strategy,
Ahab defeated Ben-hadad
in the plains and in the hills.
This was a reminder that
God is God of all places.

During the period of the two kingdoms—Judah and
Israel—the Aramean kingdom of Damascus was the
greatest enemy that Israel had. The Bible gives some
information about the wars between Israel and
Damascus (Syria), including a story about one particularly strange encounter.

Ben-hadad II of Damascus had succeeded in seiz-
ing the Galilean cities and then surrounding Samaria
with a huge army that included the chariots and
horses of some thirty-two lesser rulers fighting with
him. He sent a messenger to say to King Ahab,
"King Benhadad demands that you surrender to
him your silver and gold, your women and the
strongest of your children."

"Tell my lord, King Benhadad, that I agree; he
can have me and everything I own," Ahab
answered.

Later the messengers came back to Ahab with another demand from Benhadad: "I sent you word that you were to hand over to me your silver and gold, your women and your children. Now, however, I will send my officers to search your palace and the homes of your officials, and to take everything they consider valuable. They will be there about this time tomorrow."

(1 Kings 20:3-6 TEV)

Ahab consulted with his advisers and then sent back his answer. Although he had agreed with Ben-hadad the first time, he couldn't agree the second time. To this, Ben-hadad gave a strange reply: "I will bring enough men to destroy this city of yours and carry off the rubble in their hands. May the gods strike me dead if I don't!" (1 Kings 20:10 TEV).

King Ahab sent this message: "Tell King Ben-hadad that a real soldier does his bragging after a battle, not before it" (1 Kings 20:11 TEV). Ben-hadad received Ahab's message while he was drinking with the other rulers who had joined him.

A prophet approached Ahab at that same time and delivered the following message to Ahab: "The Lord says, 'Don't be afraid of that huge army! I will give you victory over it today, and you will know that I am the Lord' " (1 Kings 20:13 TEV).

Following the advice of the prophet, Ahab first sent a small group of men out of the besieged city. He held back his seven thousand warriors, all prepared for battle. Still drinking in his tent, the king of Damascus simply issued orders for this small group to be rounded up and captured.

Suddenly Ahab's entire army appeared out of nowhere. Ben-hadad was attacked and barely escaped; he fled on horseback, and his army abandoned arms, horses, and chariots on the battlefield. The victory went to Israel. Even so, the prophet approached Ahab again and warned him, "Go back and build up your forces and make careful plans, because the king of Syria will attack again next spring" (1 Kings 20:22 TEV).

Ben-hadad's advisors explained the reasons for their defeat by Israel by saying, "The gods of Israel are mountain gods, and that is why the Israelites defeated us. But we will certainly defeat them if we fight them in the plains" (1 Kings 20:23 TEV).

And so it was that the next year Ben-hadad assembled an army on the plain of Aphek, east of the Sea of Galilee. Once again, a prophet of God intervened and reassured Ahab,

"This is what the Lord says: 'Because the Syrians say that I am a god of the hills and not of the plains, I will give you victory over their huge army, and you and your people will know that I am the Lord.' " (1 Kings 20:28 TEV)

This time the defeat of Ben-hadad was absolute. He first hid away in the city of Aphek. Then he appeared dressed in sackcloth and with a rope around his neck and begged for his life.

King Ahab treated him with mercy. Ben-hadad had to give back to Israel the cities he had captured in the time of Omri, but then Ahab entered into a trade agreement with Ben-hadad. Later, as Ahab was passing along a road, a prophet predicted that in a future battle with Syria Ahab would be killed. The prophet said,

"This is the word of the Lord: 'Because you allowed the man to escape whom I had ordered to be killed, you will pay for it with your life, and your army will be destroyed for letting his army escape.' " (1 Kings 20:42 TEV)

23 Jehoshaphat of Judah and
Ahab of Israel were
friendly toward each other.
Together they planned
a battle against the Syrians.
Many prophets encouraged them.

Only the prophet Micaiah
wanted them not to fight.
Ahab was killed in battle.
The prophecy of Elijah
concerning Ahab
was fulfilled.

During King Ahab's reign the two kingdoms of Judah and Israel were at peace. In fact, Ahab and King Jehoshaphat of Judah were so friendly that a son of Jehoshaphat, Jehoram, married a daughter of Ahab named Athaliah.

The two kings decided to go to war together to recover the city of Ramoth-gilead, which had fallen into the hands of the Arameans. Jehoshaphat proposed that before going into battle they should ask a group of prophets what their chances might be. The prophets they consulted urged them to proceed with the war. Unfortunately, however, these prophets did not speak in the name of God; they merely told the two kings what they thought the kings wanted to hear.

There was one prophet who had not been consulted, however. Ahab hated him because he never prophesied anything good for Ahab. His name was Micaiah; he was the son of Imlah.

Jehoshaphat wanted to consult this prophet, so Micaiah was brought before the two kings seated on their thrones. All the other prophets continued enthusiastically to predict a great victory. The messenger who had gone to get Micaiah had told Micaiah that the other prophecies had been positive about the battle and that the two kings wished to have an opinion favorable to war. Micaiah made himself urge the kings to go to battle, but his heart was not in what he said. Ahab scolded him,

"When you speak to me in the name of the Lord, tell the truth! How many times do I have to tell you that?" (1 Kings 22:16 TEV)

Then Micaiah prophesied, saying, "I can see the army of Israel scattered over the hills like sheep without a shepherd. And the Lord said, 'These men have no leader; let them go home in peace.' " (1 Kings 22:17 TEV)

Ahab was furious. Nevertheless, the prophet Micaiah continued to prophesy along these lines. He claimed to have had a vision: It seemed to him as if a lying spirit had taken possession of the kings and of all of their prophets in order to deceive them and bring them to destruction. At this, one of the false prophets came forward and struck Micaiah on the face; then Ahab ordered Micaiah to be put in prison.

The kings decided to launch the war. They also decided to try a trick. Ahab put Jehoshaphat in command and dressed himself as a simple officer. He knew that the Arameans would seek first to kill him, the king of Israel; he was considered the most dangerous enemy.

In the course of the battle, however, a soldier's arrow found its way to a spot between Ahab's breastplate and his armor. Wounded, he said to his chariot driver, "Turn about, and carry me out of the battle for I am wounded" (1 Kings 22:34).

The battle raged furiously on. Ahab watched the battle while the blood flowed out of his wound all over his chariot. He was dead by evening, and the whole army took to flight. Ahab's body was carried back to Samaria, where the dogs licked the blood which had soaked the chariot, just as Elijah had prophesied.

Ahab was first succeeded by his son Ahaziah and then by his son Joram. Joram also joined with Jehoshaphat, and they won an important battle against the Moabites.

24 Elijah chose a successor,
Elisha, to continue his work
of speaking for God.
Elisha had a vision
in which Elijah did not die
but disappeared into the sky.
A tradition began that
one day Elijah would return.

When Elijah returned from the mountain where he had encountered the Lord, he busied himself, as the Lord had commanded him, with choosing a successor. Elijah chose Elisha, a rich farmer who abandoned everything when he was called to join Elijah.

Everyone knew that Elijah's work was nearing its end; soon he would return to God. Aware that this was so, Elijah wished to be alone, but Elisha would not leave him, even for an instant. Other prophets also came to see them; normally these prophets were content to follow the two of them at a distance.

One day they all reached the Jordan River. Elijah and Elisha crossed over; a group of prophets remained on the other side watching them from afar. Walking slowly, Elijah climbed up a hill. At the top he asked Elisha, ''Ask what you want before I leave you.''

Elisha replied, ''Let me inherit a double share of your spirit.''

The "double share" was the share which the eldest son usually inherited; by asking for a double share, Elisha was really asking Elijah to make him his spiritual heir and successor, the inheritor of Elijah's mission. Elijah replied,

"That is a difficult request to grant. But you will receive it if you see me as I am being taken away from you; if you don't see me, you won't receive it." (2 Kings 2:10 TEV)

By these words Elijah meant that it was not up to him to grant Elisha's request; it was up to the Lord. The sign that God was in favor of it would be that Elisha would be able to see Elijah's departure.

As the two prophets walked along, Elisha suddenly had a vision: he saw a chariot of fire drawn by horses of fire that came between him and Elijah; Elijah was taken up on the chariot and disappeared into the sky. Elisha saw, and cried out, "My father,

my father! Mighty defender of Israel! You are gone!" (2 Kings 2:12 TEV).

Then he saw nothing more. The mantle of Elijah had fallen off and was left to Elisha, as the sign that Elijah's spirit had come to rest on him too. Elisha took up the mantle and turned back towards the Jordan. It was immediately apparent to all that Elisha had inherited Elijah's spirit. Elisha was now capable of performing miracles, just as Elijah had been.

The mystery of Elijah's strange disappearance was always remembered among the Chosen People. Many said that Elijah had not actually died; they said that at the moment when a great spiritual guide became most needed, Elijah would come back.

25 Many stories in the Bible tell
about Elisha's miracles.
In one, a woman who had had
no children bore a child.
When the boy died,
Elisha restored him to life.

The prophet Elisha became famous for the many miracles that he performed. One of the stories told about Elisha greatly resembles an incident that occurred in Elijah's life. It took place in the city of Shunem, where a wealthy family used to offer generous hospitality to Elisha whenever he passed through. The wife and her husband prepared a second-floor room for Elisha and furnished it for his use. Elisha wanted to do something for the woman in return, but the woman humbly refused. Then Elisha thought of a way to show his gratitude. Aware that the couple had no child, Elisha called the woman in to him and told her, ''By this time next year you will be holding a son in your arms'' (2 Kings 4:16 TEV). And, in fact, to everyone's surprise, that was what happened.

Some years later, tragedy struck. The little boy ran out to join his father, who was working among the reapers; when he reached his father, he began to complain of a terrible headache. The boy was taken to his mother who held him in her lap without being able to do anything for him. Around noon the little boy died.

The woman took the dead child upstairs and laid him out on the bed of the prophet of God. Then she had a donkey saddled, and she left to go find Elisha, who was in another city. When Elisha saw her coming, he sent his servant to meet her to inquire whether anything had happened. The servant asked her, ''Are you all right? Is your husband? Is your child?''

The woman said that all was well. But when she came before Elisha, she threw herself, sobbing, at his feet. The servant, not understanding, tried to

He lay down on the boy, placing his mouth, eyes, and hands on the boy's mouth, eyes and hands. As he lay stretched out over the boy, the boy's body started to get warm. (2 Kings 4:34 TEV)

The little boy opened his eyes and stood up as if he had merely been sleeping. Elisha took him downstairs and returned him to his mother.

Many other stories were told about Elisha's miracles. On one occasion, like Elijah, he kept replenishing the oil in the jar of a poor widow threatened by creditors. On another occasion, during a famine, he changed a stew that had been made of poisonous plants into a healthful and tasty food. On still another occasion, he multiplied some loaves of bread until there was enough to feed a hundred men.

Through all these wondrous acts, God showed the people that Elisha was his true prophet. Only then would the people listen to Elisha when he declared the word of God.

push her away, but the prophet stopped him, saying, ''Leave her alone. She's very upset. The Lord has not told me anything about it.''

The woman scolded Elisha. ''I didn't ask you for a son. Why did you get my hopes up?''

Elisha sent his servant hurrying back to the woman's house; the servant was told to lay the prophet's staff across the child's body. However, the woman begged Elisha to come in person, so together they started back. On the way, the servant returned to report that laying the staff across the child hadn't helped.

When Elisha arrived at the woman's house, he closed himself in the room with the dead child and did the same thing that Elijah had done earlier in a similar situation.

26 Elisha's most famous miracle
was curing a Syrian general.
The Syrian, Naaman, was told
by Elisha to bathe in the Jordan.
At first he refused,
but then he obeyed.
This foreign soldier came
to consider Elisha's God
the one true God.

Perhaps the most famous of Elisha's miracles was the one he performed on behalf of a foreigner. It happened this way. One of the bravest generals in the Aramean kingdom of Syria was a man called Naaman. Naaman had developed the dread disease of leprosy. One day a slave girl of Israelite origin who served Naaman's wife told her mistress that there was a prophet in Israel who could cure Naaman's leprosy. When the Syrian king learned this, he decided to send Naaman to Samaria, along with a personal letter to the king of Israel. The message written in the letter said:

"When this letter reaches you, know that I have sent to you Naaman, my servant, that you may cure him of his leprosy." (2 Kings 5:6)

When the king of Israel read this letter, he tore his clothes. (At that time, tearing one's clothes was a common gesture of desperation.) The Israelite king thought that the letter was only an excuse: If he was unable to do this impossible thing, then the Syrian king would have an excuse for attacking Israel in spite of the treaty of peace that existed. "Does he think I'm God, able to grant life or death?" the poor king demanded. "He's just trying to start trouble."

When Elisha learned what was going on in the royal court, he sent word to the king.

"Why are you so upset? Send the man to me, and I'll show him that there is a prophet in Israel!" (2 Kings 5:8 TEV)

So Naaman the Syrian was sent to Elisha. The general arrived at the prophet's house in his ornate chariot, accompanied by his richly dressed followers. But the prophet merely sent his servant out to tell the Syrian general,

"Go and wash in the Jordan seven times, and your flesh shall be restored, and you shall be clean." (2 Kings 5:10)

Naaman had expected to be welcomed and treated with respect. He was furious at Elisha's casual treatment of him.

"Behold, I thought that he would surely come out to me, and stand, and call on the name of the Lord his God, and wave his hand over the place and cure the leper. Are not Abana and Pharpar, the rivers of Damascus, better than all the waters of Israel? Could I not wash in them and be clean? (2 Kings 5:11-12)

Naaman turned his chariot around and went away. However, some of his followers finally succeeded in calming him down. They said to him, with great common sense,

"Sir, if the prophet had told you to do something difficult, you would have done it. Now why can't you just wash yourself, as he said, and be cured?" (2 Kings 5:13 TEV)

Naaman knew that he had been foolishly proud, so he went down to the Jordan and bathed himself in it seven times. His flesh then became healthy and smooth, like the flesh of a little baby. With that, the Syrian general bowed down before the prophet of God—and before the God of the prophet.

Naaman wished to give lavish gifts to Elisha, but the prophet refused to accept anything. So Naaman asked for a gift for himself: He asked to be able to take away with him as much of the earth of Israel as two mules could carry. Since he had come to consider Elisha's God the one true God, he wanted to have a portion of Elisha's holy ground on which to worship God, wherever he was.

Word of this miracle spread among the people. Other miracles even stranger were told about him. One day, while cutting down a tree on the bank of the Jordan, the son of another prophet lost the iron head of his axe in the water. Elisha threw a stick into the river where the axe head had fallen in, and the iron tool floated up to the surface.

27 King Ben-hadad II of Syria
attacked Israel again
and besieged Samaria.
When Israel was about
to surrender,
Syria mysteriously retreated.
The Bible says Israel's victory
was the work of God.

After the death of Ahab and the death of his oldest
son and successor Ahaziah, who had a very brief
reign, another son of Ahab's—Joram—became
king of Israel. Joram reigned from 852 to 841 B.C.
During his reign, Ben-hadad II, king of Damascus
in Syria, continued his wars for territory against
Israel. Eventually, Ben-hadad set up a siege of the
city of Samaria itself.

The people inside of Samaria resisted the siege for
months and months, until they were nearly out of
food. When the animals usually slaughtered for food
were all gone, they began to kill their mules and their
horses, even though horses were needed for warfare.
A donkey's head was selling for eighty pieces of
silver—a great price. There were even cases of
cannibalism.

King Joram was desperate. He bitterly resented
Elisha, who had advised him to resist and had
promised that God would be with him. So one day,
Joram went to Elisha's house to arrest him and have
him put to death. The king said to Elisha,

"It's the Lord who has brought this trouble on us! Why should I wait any longer for him to do something?"

Elisha answered, "Listen to what the Lord says! By this time tomorrow you will be able to buy in Samaria ten pounds of the best wheat or twenty pounds of barley for one piece of silver."

The personal attendant of the king said to Elisha, "That can't happen—not even if the Lord himself were to send grain at once!"

(2 Kings 6:33-7:2 TEV)

That same evening some lepers who stood outside the city gates, themselves weak from hunger, decided to go over to the Syrian camp to seek food. The Syrians might kill them, but they were going to die of hunger anyway, they reasoned.

When they reached the Syrian camp after sunset, however, they discovered that it had been abandoned. There were no guards, no voices, no camp noises. They crept into one of the tents, where they found some food and could finally eat. They also discovered gold and other precious objects, which they carried away to hide. Then they cautiously returned and examined some other tents; they took other valuables, and eventually they realized that no one at all was left in the Syrian camp.

What had happened? The Bible says that the Lord had caused the sounds of chariots, hoofbeats, and other noises of a great army to be heard all around the camp. The Syrians feared that the kings of the Hittites or the Egyptians had ridden to the aid of the king of Israel. Terrified, they all fled towards the Jordan, abandoning their camp just as it was.

After having hidden away even more booty, the lepers returned to Samaria to announce the good news that the Syrian camp had been abandoned. At first the king suspected some kind of trap had been set by the Syrians. But some of his officers, riding off in chariots drawn by horses that were practically skeletons, confirmed that the army had indeed fled; its trail was littered with clothing and equipment left behind in haste.

The good news spread in a flash, and by morning a throng of people had moved in to sack the Syrian camp. A market sprang up suddenly at the city gates, selling merchandise from the camp. The king put in charge there the captain who had earlier been doubtful about Elisha's prophecy. In the market's turmoil and confusion, the captain was trampled to death by the crowds—but not before seeing with his own eyes, as the prophet had predicted, both a measure of fine meal and two measures of barley selling for a single silver piece.

28 Because of the evil of
the royal family,
Elisha anointed as king
a general named Jehu.
Jehu led a successful revolt
against Joram, Ahab's son.
Joram's mother, Jezebel,
was thrown from a window.
Her death fulfilled the
prophecy of Elijah.

The prophet Elisha had been chosen, as had Elijah before him, to defend the true religion of the Israelites. Elisha decided that he must put to an end the dynasty of Omri because Omri and his sons had persisted in worshiping false gods and idols, bringing evil to Israel. Omri's dynasty had reached its most evil point when Ahab and Jezebel reigned. Now Ahab and Jezebel's son, King Joram, was continuing in their pagan ways.

In obedience to a commandment of God Elisha one day sent a follower of his to Ramoth-gilead to seek out the Israelite commander there, a general named Jehu. The prophet's disciple called Jehu aside and then poured a flask of oil over his head to anoint him. (The Israelites' kings were consecrated to God through anointing.) The disciple announced to Jehu, as Elisha had instructed him, "Thus says the Lord, 'I anoint you King over Israel'" (2 Kings 9:3). The disciple departed without waiting to answer any questions, again as Elisha had instructed him.

What Jehu understood from this was that God had decided to abandon the house of Omri and Ahab, stained with so many crimes. The punishments that had been prophesied against Jezebel were about to take place.

When Jehu told his fellow officers what had happened, they immediately acclaimed him their king; they set themselves up in rebellion against King Joram. Jehu, however, swore them to secrecy for the moment. Then he led some of his troops out towards Jezreel, the city in which Joram had taken refuge. When Joram saw Jehu coming, he sent messengers out to meet Jehu and learn the reasons for this sudden appearance. But each messenger in turn joined Jehu and did not come back. Shortly afterwards, Jehu set out in his chariot to meet Joram. With Joram, in another chariot, was Ahaziah, the king of Judah, who had come to visit.

"Are you coming in peace?" Joram asked him.

"How can there be peace," Jehu answered, "when we still have all the witchcraft and idolatry that your mother Jezebel started?"

(2 Kings 9:22 TEV)

Immediately realizing that Jehu was rebelling against his rule, Joram turned his chariot around to flee. But Jehu drew his bow and shot the king between the shoulders. Jehu's arrow pierced his heart and he fell dead in his chariot. A soldier took his body and threw it down into the nearby field.

The other king, Ahaziah, was also wounded as he fled. He died, and his men took him to Jerusalem where they buried him in the royal tombs.

Meanwhile, Jehu entered the city of Jezreel. When Jezebel caught sight of him coming, she put on eye shadow and did up her hair, hoping to charm him when he came into the royal palace. When Jehu passed by, she called to him from a window. He ordered her thrown down from the window. This was done, and Jezebel's blood splashed on the walls and on the horses as Jehu and his party passed by.

A little later, the new king gave the order for Jezebel's body to be buried, but it was reported back to him that her body had been devoured by dogs. In this way, Elijah's prophecy about Jezebel was fulfilled: "In the territory of Jezreel the dogs shall eat the flesh of Jezebel" (2 Kings 9:36).

Elisha lived to see all the prophecies of Elijah fulfilled. In fact, he lived even longer; he lived into the reign of Jehu's grandson, Jehoash. This king wept by Elisha's deathbed, saying, "My father, my father, you have greatly defended Israel." Before his death, Elisha advised Jehoash to stop fighting wars with Israel's main enemy, Syria.

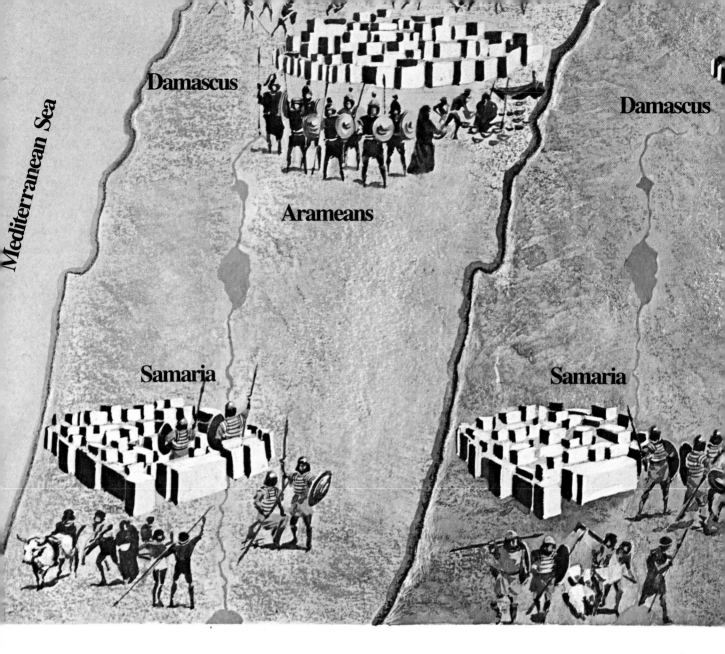

Mediterranean Sea

Damascus

Arameans

Samaria

Damascus

Samaria

29 Israel (or Samaria)
faced two hostile powers
to the north: Assyria,
and Syria (or Damascus).
In the end, Assyria controlled
both Syria and Israel.

Syria, with its major city of Damascus, was at the height of its power during the reigns of Jehu (841-814 B.C.) and his son Jehoahaz (814-798 B.C.) in Israel. The Assyrian leader, Shalmaneser III (858-824 B.C.), repeatedly sent expeditions against Damascus and other kings supporting Damascus, but Damascus was strong enough to overcome Assyria's efforts at conquest.

On one of these expeditions, in 853 B.C., Shalmaneser III led his army west from Assyria toward the Mediterranean. The Syrian king, Ben-hadad II, gathered a group of local kings to fight Assyria. Ben-hadad supplied 20,000 infantry; and Ahab of Israel, his ally during this venture, provided 2,000 chariots, as well as 10,000 foot soldiers. The alliance of twelve kings under Damascus fought Shalmaneser at Qarqar, on the Syrian river called Orontes, and they managed to stop him there.

In an inscription on an Assyrian monument which remains today from that long-ago time, Shalmaneser brags that he won a victory over twelve kings. In fact, however, it was not really a victory. He returned home and did not come back to the area for twelve years.

When Shalmaneser did return, in 841 B.C., Jehu was king in Israel and Hazael ruled in Syria. Hazael had been a general of Ben-hadad II's. Once when Elisha was passing through Damascus, the sick King Ben-hadad II sent his commander, Hazael, to ask the "man of God" whether he would be cured or not. Elisha gave a strange reply: The king would

Damascus

Assyrians

Assyrians

Samaria

recover but was about to die. Elisha also told Hazael that he himself would one day be the king of Damascus. The prophet wept as he predicted the evil that Hazael would do to Israel: "You will set on fire their fortresses, and you will slay their young men with the sword, and dash in pieces their little ones, and rip up their women with child" (2 Kings 8:12).

It happened as Elisha said it would. Hazael killed Ben-hadad II and became king of Syria. During Jehu's reign in Israel, Hazael repeatedly attacked the Israelite border garrisons, occupied all the Israelite territory east of the Jordan, and massacred the civilian populations there.

Jehu was succeeded by his son Jehoahaz, who fought continual wars with the son of Hazael, Ben-hadad III. At the end of these wars, the king of Israel had in his army only "fifty horsemen, ten chariots, and ten thousand men on foot" (2 Kings 13:7 TEV). Jehoahaz prayed to the Lord and then the Lord "gave Israel a savior, so that they escaped from the hand of the Syrians" (2 Kings 13:5). This savior turned out to be the Assyrian emperor, Adad-nirari III, who besieged Damascus, giving some relief to Israel.

Next on the throne of Israel was Jehoash (798-783 B.C.). Elisha, just before his own death, prophesied a victory Jehoash would have over Syria. The prophet ordered the king to draw his bow and shoot an arrow eastwards. Elisha called the arrow "the Lord's arrow of victory, the arrow of victory over Syria!" (2 Kings 13:17).

Then Elisha told Jehoash to strike the ground with his bundle of arrows. Jehoash struck the ground three times and stopped. Greatly disappointed, Elisha told Jehoash, "You should have struck five or six times; then you would have struck down Syria until you had made an end of it, but now you will strike down Syria only three times" (2 Kings 13:19). As it turned out, Jehoash defeated Ben-hadad III three times and reconquered the territory that Hazael had taken from Israel.

30 While Jeroboam II was king,
from 783 to 743 B.C.,
the northern kingdom of Israel
reached its greatest
power and prosperity.
But idolatry and injustice
weakened the kingdom.

With the victory of King Jehoash over Ben-hadad III of Syria, and the return of Israel's lost territories across the Jordan, the northern kingdom was not only freed from being subject to Damascus, but it also regained its position as a great power. Israel's strength at this time was seen in the proud manner in which Jehoash treated Amaziah, king of Judah. Amaziah, grown bold by a victory over the Edomites, tried to pick a quarrel with Israel. However, Jehoash responded to Judah's challenge with this message:

"Once a thorn bush on the Lebanon Mountains sent a message to a cedar: 'Give your daughter in marriage to my son.' A wild animal passed by and trampled the bush down."

(2 Kings 14:9 TEV)

The huge cedar towering over the lowly thistle was intended to represent the king of Israel compared to Amaziah of Judah. Jehoash advised Amaziah to remain where he was, and not attempt to make himself equal to Israel.

Amaziah did not take this advice, and war eventually did break out. Jehoash defeated Amaziah overwhelmingly and took him prisoner; Jehoash

went on to Jerusalem, destroyed part of the city walls, carried off the gold and silver in the Temple and the royal palace, and returned to Samaria with hostages from Judah.

During the forty-year reign of Jeroboam II, the son of Jehoash, Israel's power and splendor reached its highest point since Solomon. Jeroboam II re-established the same borders that Solomon had in the north, and he made Damascus subject to him. Free from outside attack, the agriculture of Israel once again flowered and trade prospered. There was much new building construction in the capital, Samaria, just as in the time of Omri and Ahab.

Amos, a famous prophet at that time, found it necessary to scold the rich for their luxurious ways of living. He spoke of the great palaces and "houses of ivory," with carved ivory decorations on their walls and furnishings. It was a time of great wealth for Samaria, at least for the nobles and for others enriched by the development of trade and agriculture. Amos warned:

"How terrible it will be for you that stretch out on your luxurious couches, feasting on veal and lamb! You like to compose songs, as David did, and play them on harps. You drink wine by the bowlful and use the finest perfumes, but you do not mourn over the ruin of Israel. So you will be the first to go into exile. Your feasts and banquets will come to an end." (Amos 6:4-7 TEV)

The wealth and security of Israel in this period were certainly a sign of efficient government administration and military power. The danger of Assyria seemed far away, for the reign of Jeroboam II corresponded to a period of Assyrian weakness. Assyria had temporarily stopped making further conquests in the west.

However, while there was great wealth in Israel, there was also great injustice being done to the poor. And there was little true worship of God, for the nation was given to luxurious living and the worship of false gods.

31 Amos, a fruit-gatherer
and shepherd, discovered
God's call to be a prophet.
He foretold the downfall
of the rich but corrupt
kingdom of Israel.
Punishment would come
for their idolatry and
their mistreatment of the poor.

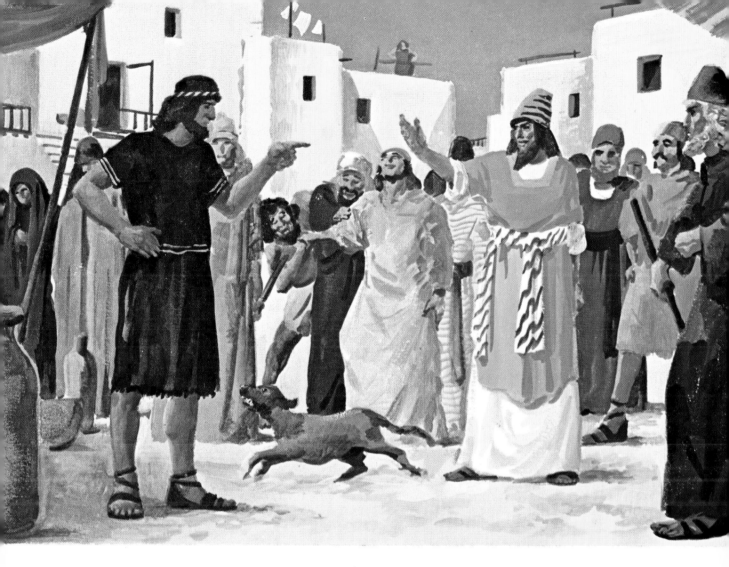

The kingdom of Israel reached its greatest splendor and power during the reign of King Jeroboam II. But as the rich grew more wealthy, the poorer people became worse off. God sent a new prophet—Amos—to warn that an unjust society like Israel was bound to collapse.

Amos was a shepherd from Judah, who received his call from God while he was tending his flocks and gathering the fruit of sycamore trees. God's call to Amos, like God's call to the other prophets, was strong and irresistible. God had given Amos a sudden, clear vision of Israel's true social and political situation: Although everything seemed outwardly splendid in Israel, Israel was really like very ripe fruit in a basket—the fruit look beautiful, but they are on the verge of beginning to rot.

Amos was from Judah, but he felt called to speak in Israel. He began to proclaim the word of the Lord in the squares and public places of the city of Bethel. Bethel contained one of the sanctuaries where the Israelites went to worship God.

Amos spoke to the people about all of Israel's neighboring countries; he spelled out how God would punish each one for its misdeeds. Even closer to Amos' heart, however, were the Israelite people. They should have been closest to the God who had chosen them, but they had become, in fact, more corrupt than the other nations. Amos pointed out that God did not want the external rituals of organized religion; the people tried to please God with these, and meanwhile they went right on breaking God's law. Amos scolded those who lived in proud, shameless luxury that was made possible only by the sufferings of the poor. He warned that those who lived such rich, frivolous lives, without any thought for anyone else, had a false sense of security and would bring ruin to the whole nation.

Amos shared with the people of Israel his series of visions of the punishment that was close at hand. The punishment would be like a plague of locusts falling upon and devouring the crops; it would be like a city when all its buildings fell down. With each one of these visions, Amos prayed to God to pardon the people of Israel.

"Sovereign Lord, forgive your people! How can they survive? They are so small and weak!"

(Amos 7:2 TEV)

God had continually pardoned Israel, but punishment was now sure to come. This was the message that Amos cried in the squares and streets of Bethel, and later on in Samaria.

Because of the message that he delivered, Amos is often considered the prophet of social justice; he admonished the rich and defended the poor. It is true that Amos expressed ideas that today we consider important in regard to social justice, but he did not speak out merely because of his own ideas or out of his anger. He spoke out because of his vivid sense of what God had done for his Chosen People and his unhappy awareness of how much they had forgotten and betrayed God.

32 God condemned the rich
for not caring about the poor
and for believing that
offerings and ceremonies alone
would please God.
Many listeners were furious
when Amos spoke.

The biblical Book of Amos contains some of the words of Amos, the first prophet whose message was written down. His words lash out against injustice. For him, injustice meant to forget and oppress one's neighbor—because this meant to forget the God who is the guardian over all. Amos, speaking for God, attacked those who thought they could please God by their offerings and their religious festivals:

"I hate, I despise your feasts,
    and I take no delight
        in your solemn assemblies.
Even though you bring me your burnt
        offerings and cereal offerings,
    I will not accept them,
and the peace offerings of your
        fatted beasts
    I will not look upon.
Take away from me the noise of your songs;
    to the melody of your harps
        I will not listen.
But let justice roll down like waters,
    and righteousness like an everflowing
        stream."
                    (Amos 5:21-24)

Amos condemns the rich and the noble who, although they could have some influence over the destiny of the nation, instead go on living only for their own pleasures. And so Amos accuses the rich of feathering their own nests at the expense of the weakest and poorest of people.

"You people hate anyone who challenges injustice and speaks the whole truth in court. You have oppressed the poor and robbed them of their grain. And so you will not live in the fine stone houses you build or drink wine from the beautiful vineyards you plant. I know how terrible your sins are and how many crimes you have committed. You persecute good men, take bribes, and prevent the poor from getting justice in the courts." (Amos 5:10-12 TEV)

Amos warned that those who acted without heeding God's law would come to a bad end. His words angered the rich and powerful. One of the principal priests of Bethel, Amaziah, denounced Amos to King Jeroboam II, accusing the prophet of conspiring against the king. Amos was forced to leave Bethel.

In the meantime, though, the people had heard the terrible prophecy of Amos that Samaria would be destroyed. It was to the priest Amaziah that Amos prophesied in these words:

Amos answered, "I am not the kind of prophet who prophesies for pay. I am a herdsman, and I take care of fig trees. But the Lord took me from my work as a shepherd and ordered me to go and prophesy to his people Israel. So now listen to what the Lord says. You tell me to stop prophesying, to stop raving against the people of Israel. And so, Amaziah, the Lord says to you, 'Your wife will become a prostitute in the city, and your children will be killed in war. Your land will be divided up and given to others, and you yourself will die in a heathen country. And the people of Israel will certainly be taken away from their own land into exile.'" (Amos 7:14-17 TEV)

Many were furious at Amos on account of this prophecy. Some of his listeners realized that the prophet was announcing the fall of Samaria and the exile of the people.

Along with his many dreadful predictions, Amos also promised that God would not abandon his people completely. One day God would reunite and save them, in spite of everything.

33 The prophet Hosea loved
and was faithful to his wife,
although she was unfaithful to him.
Hosea said that Israel
was like an unfaithful wife.
They were forsaking God
and their covenant with him
in order to worship idols.

Toward the end of the reign of Jeroboam II, another prophet arose in Israel. He was Hosea, son of Beeri. Like Amos, he prophesied imminent catastrophe for the northern kingdom. There would be military defeat, ruin, and deportation of the people, according to Hosea.

Hosea and Amos, however, probably never met. Certainly their styles of writing were very different. The prophecies of Amos are short compositions, written in verse, easily memorized. The prophecies of Hosea are much more fully developed, both in their writing and in their thought.

Hosea's idea of God seems more like the idea we have of God today. Hosea understood that God did not limit himself merely to punishing sinners; God had pity on them and loved them, even though they were sinners. Confronted with sinners, God seemed to Hosea to be almost of two minds, undecided whether his anger or his love should win out. God's love is what the prophet Hosea stressed. More than any other prophet, he understood that God is love, and he expressed this idea throughout his prophecies.

Hosea used an unhappy situation in his own life to illustrate in his preaching the force of God's love for his people. Hosea was married to Gomer, who turned out to be an unfaithful wife. In spite of Gomer's adultery, Hosea forgave her and took her back.

Hosea's experience with Gomer influenced his idea of the Lord's relationship with his people. He compared Israel to a wife betraying her husband; Israel had abandoned God and had been unfaithful to the Lord by taking part in pagan cults, with their worship of alien gods. The people had forgotten God, the one who had loved them and brought them out of Egypt. But just as the prophet refused to abandon his wife even though she was unfaithful, so God would not forever abandon his people.

This is one of the main messages of Hosea's prophecy: Love is stronger than infidelity. At the same time that Hosea declares God's punishment, he gives his listeners a hope of salvation.

34 Hosea attacked the priests
who forgot the law of God.
Hosea said that God loved
his people Israel
but would punish them
to bring them back to him.
God did not want
to punish his Chosen People
but to show them his goodness.
God said to Israel,
"I want your constant love,
not your animal sacrifices."

In his preaching, Hosea battled mightily against the Israelites' idolatry. The covenant with God was repeatedly broken by the widespread worship of false gods in the "high places," the local shrines on hilltops and under sacred trees. Through the mouth of his prophet, God told the people,

"My people have broken the covenant I made with them and have rebelled against my teaching. Even though they call me their God and claim that they are my people and that they know me, they have rejected what is good. Because of this their enemies will pursue them." (Hosea 8:1-3 TEV)

The priests especially, according to Hosea, were the ones who should have taught the people the true nature of God and the requirements of God's law and living according to his covenant. However, the priests themselves neglected God's law. They permitted swearing, lying, stealing, killing, and adultery. How could the sacrifice of a few animals counteract such evils as those? God rejected those kinds of sacrifices; both the priests and people who belonged to such cults deserved God's punishment.

If only Israel could see clearly again, even for a moment; if only the people would express true feelings of repentance; if only they would return to God. If they did that, God would lavish on them his pity and tenderness.

It was as if God were questioning himself, asking himself the best way to deal with his people. God loved Israel deeply. His punishment was meant to bring the people back to him—to make them once again God's people and not unfaithful people, straying away after false gods.

Here the Bible records the dialogue between God and his people:

The people say, "Let's return to the Lord! He has hurt us, but he will be sure to heal us; he has wounded us, but he will bandage our wounds, won't he? In two or three days he will revive us, and we will live in his presence. Let us try to know the Lord. He will come to us as surely as the day dawns, as surely as the spring rains fall upon the earth."

But the Lord says, "Israel and Judah, what am I going to do with you? Your love for me disappears as quickly as morning mist; it is like dew, that vanishes early in the day. That is why I have sent my prophets to you with my message of judgment and destruction. What I want from you is plain and clear: I want your constant love, not your animal sacrifices. I would rather have my people know me than have them burn offerings to me.

"But as soon as they entered the land at Adam, they broke the covenant I had made with them. Gilead is a city full of evil men and murderers. The priests are like a gang of robbers who wait in ambush for a man. Even on the road to the holy place at Shechem they commit murder. And they do all this evil deliberately! I have seen a horrible thing in Israel: my people have defiled themselves by worshiping idols.

"And as for you, people of Judah, I have set a time to punish you also for what you are doing."

(Hosea 6 TEV)

35 As a parent loves a child,
so God loves Israel, saying
"I taught Israel to walk.
I picked him up and
held him to my cheek.
How can I abandon you, Israel?
My love for you is too strong."

The Lord says,
"When Israel was a child, I loved him
    and called him out of Egypt as my son.
But the more I called to him,
    the more he turned away from me.
My people sacrificed to Baal;
    they burned incense to idols.
Yet I was the one who taught Israel to walk.
I took my people up in my arms,
    but they did not acknowledge that I
        took care of them.
I drew them to me with affection and love.
    I picked them up and held
        them to my cheek;
    I bent down to them and fed them.

"They refuse to return to me, and so they must
return to Egypt, and Assyria will rule them. War will
sweep through their cities and break down the city
gates. It will destroy my people because they do
what they themselves think best. They insist on
turning away from me. They will cry out because of
the yoke that is on them, but no one will lift it from
them.

"How can I give you up, Israel?
    How can I abandon you?
Could I ever destroy you as I did Admah,
    or treat you as I did Zeboiim?
My heart will not let me do it!
    My love for you is too strong.
I will not punish you in my anger;
    I will not destroy Israel again.
For I am God and not man.
    I, the Holy One, am with you.
I will not come to you in anger.

"My people will follow me when I roar like a lion
at their enemies. They will hurry to me from the
west. They will come from Egypt, as swiftly as
birds, and from Assyria, like doves. I will bring
them to their homes again. I, the Lord, have
spoken." (Hosea 11:1-11 TEV)

36 Between 850 and 700 B.C.
the southern kingdom, Judah,
like Israel to the north,
had many weak rulers and
plots among its leaders.
Still, there were some
who remained faithful to God.

So far in this book we have been reading mostly about the fortunes of the northern kingdom of Israel; in this chapter, we will begin to look at the southern kingdom of Judah. Judah was small, but it possessed as its capital Jerusalem, the holy city. The Temple built by Solomon was there. So was the royal palace in which descendants of David still reigned.

The last king of Judah we read about was Jehoshaphat. After his death in 848 B.C., more than a century passed before another king of equal importance came to the throne. This king was Hezekiah, who ascended the throne in 716 B.C. This chapter presents a brief review of the kings who sat on the throne of David between 849 and 716 B.C.

Jehoram, the son and successor of Jehoshaphat, married Athaliah, the daughter of King Ahab and Queen Jezebel of Israel. During his reign, relations between the southern and northern kingdoms were quite good, although they would not remain that way. They took a turn for the worse when Ahaziah, Jehoram's son and successor, traveled to Israel to visit King Ahab. While there, he was killed when Jehu took Israel's throne from King Ahab.

The queen mother, Athaliah, took advantage of the situation. In order to seize the throne for herself, she ordered all the members of the royal family to be killed. However, one member, the child prince,

Joash, was hidden away with a priest, Jehoiada, in the Temple. Six years later Jehoiada decided the time was ripe for the coronation of Joash as the legitimate ruler in place of his mother. He arranged for Joash to be crowned king in the Temple, in front of crowds of people and under the royal guards' protection.

Athaliah, who lived nearby in the royal palace, heard the trumpet blasts and shouts and rushed to the Temple. The guards immediately took hold of her, dragged her outside the Temple area, and killed her.

Then Jehoiada had the people and King Joash renew their covenant with God, in order to celebrate the restoration of David's line on the throne. The people smashed the altars of Baal set up by Athaliah. After years of pagan infiltration, the pure worship of the true God was renewed, and the Temple building was restored.

King Joash kept the kingdom on the right path so long as the priest Jehoiada lived, but after his death, Joash fell under the influence of bad counselors. The worship of idols began again in Judah. When Zechariah, the son of Jehoiada, prophesied against this new betrayal of God, he was stoned to death.

Joash's death came under mysterious circumstances, after a defeat by the Syrians. The king was killed in a plot organized by his own men. In spite of that, his son Amaziah succeeded him on the throne of Judah—and then arranged to have killed all those who had plotted against his father. Amaziah was strong and energetic. He defeated the Edomites in battle—but then he was defeated in turn by the king of Israel. In his old age a plot was hatched against him, and he fled to Lachish, thirty miles from Jerusalem. He was pursued there and killed.

Amaziah was succeeded by his son Uzziah, also called Azariah. His rule was a prosperous and lengthy one, extending from 781 to 740 B.C. He was stricken with leprosy during his reign, however, and shared his rule with his son Jotham. Jotham ascended the throne around 740 B.C. This was about the time that Tiglath-pileser III, the great Assyrian conquerer, came to power. It was only by paying a heavy tribute to Assyria that Ahaz, the son of Jotham, was able to remain king.

These were the external events in the kingdom of Judah between 849 and 716 B.C. It was a history of weakness and constant plots against the throne, a history much like other small kingdoms in the Near East. The difference between Judah and these other minor kingdoms lay in the hearts of those few Israelites who preserved the worship of the true God. They kept alive the hope of the salvation promised by God.

37 King Uzziah of Judah
ruled in a time of prosperity.
He promoted agriculture
and the raising of animals,
the building of defense towers,
and the digging of wells.

The southern kingdom of Judah, like Israel to the north, had to deal with the great power that threatened from the north, the Assyrian Empire. But from around 780 to 740 B.C. Assyria passed through a period of weakness caused by internal conflicts. It was during this time that the kingdom of Israel enjoyed its greatest power, under King Jeroboam II. During this same time, the kingdom of Judah also became quite prosperous under King Uzziah.

Uzziah's father had been assassinated by two conspirators; he ascended the throne at age seventeen. Since he did not have to worry about threats from the north, from either Israel or Assyria, he turned his attention to the south. He reconquered and rebuilt the harbor city and copper-smelting center, Elath, on the Gulf of Aqaba. He also conquered some of the principal cities of the Philistines: Gath, Jabneh, and Ashdod.

Uzziah worked at developing agriculture. He encouraged raising animals and planting vineyards. The Bible says of him:

"He also built fortified towers in the open country and dug many cisterns, because he had large

herds of cattle in the western foothills and plains. Because he loved farming, he encouraged the people to plant vineyards in the hill country and to farm the fertile land.'' (2 Chronicles 26:10 TEV) These products were sold to neighboring peoples; it was from this that Judah's wealth and prosperity came. Using that wealth, Uzziah undertook a widespread construction program, both military and civilian. He built new towers on the walls of Jerusalem, at the Corner Gate, Valley Gate, and Angle Gate. He built fortified towers in the desert plains south of the country. He also had dug a string of wells and cisterns, which were very useful in raising animals.

To defend this prosperity from the attacks of enemies, Uzziah also reinforced the army. He supplied it with arms and weapons that must have been the most modern of the times: ''Shields, spears, helmets, coats of mail, bows, and stones for slings'' (2 Chronicles 26:14). In Jerusalem, he installed huge devices to launch stones and arrows.

The little kingdom of Judah was thus both prosperous and in a high state of preparedness. As far away as Egypt and even farther, the kingdom was spoken of with admiration.

However, this well-being did not last. Probably the reasons for the kingdom's decline were many. The Bible, of course, gives a religious explanation. The people of Judah had had increasing contact with the surrounding peoples, such as the Philistines; they ended up by adopting many of the idols and practices of these peoples. More than that, they tended to follow the example set by the king. King Uzziah had the idea that he himself should be offering religious sacrifice, like many of the neighboring kings. One day he entered the Temple. Disregarding the warnings of the priests that only the sons of Aaron were permitted to enter the sanctuary to offer sacrifice to God, he went ahead and did it himself. He dismissed the priests angrily. Soon after he developed the dread disease, leprosy.

From then on, Uzziah lived off by himself in a palace tower, and shared his rule with his son Jotham. And so ended Uzziah's reign, a king who had brought such economic well-being and military power to Judah.

Rome

Athens

Sparta

38 These are some
of the centers of civilization
in the eastern Mediterranean Sea
around 750 B.C.

Italy

In the midst of small villages where Latin shepherds
lived, a small, walled city was growing up on the
Palatine Hill. It was called Rome. In later years the
foundation of the city would be dated to 753 B.C.
Nobody among the population there at that time, not
even the Etruscan soothsayers who had established
themselves south of the Apennine Mountains, had
any idea of the future glory of Rome.

Greece

Around 750 B.C. Greece was just emerging out of
the period of prehistory and legend. Rivalry and
disunity were widespread among the various tribes
gathered into small city-states. One of these city-
states, Sparta, was getting ready to colonize the toe
of Italy. Sparta was governed according to unwritten
laws attributed to the ninth-century lawgiver,
Lycurgus. The city-state of Athens, meanwhile, had
unified the territory called Attica. The monarchy had
been abolished and Athens was governed by officials called "archons." Later Athens was called the
world's first democracy. Meanwhile, Greek sea-
farers were establishing colonies in southern Italy
and Sicily.

Egypt

Between 740 and 730 B.C., Egypt was weak. In the
Nile Delta the twenty-third dynasty (748-730 B.C.)
had no authority over the local rulers (generals or
priests), who governed independently. But at Sais,
near the Nile Delta, Tefnakht (twenty-fourth dynasty, 730-715 B.C.) tried to impose his authority.
During the same period, another Egyptian state was
growing up 800 miles to the south at Napata, in
Nubia. King Piankhi of Napata eventually, around
730, began the conquest of all of Egypt; he founded
the twenty-fifth dynasty (751-565 B.C.), also called
the Ethiopian dynasty, under which Egypt would be
defeated by Assyria.

Assyrians

Isaiah

Sais

Thebes

Israel

The troubles that would bring to an end the northern kingdom began at the death of Jeroboam II in 743 B.C. Zechariah, his son, was killed after the briefest of reigns, and so was Shallum, the person who had seized Zechariah's throne. The reign of Menahem began next.

Judah

After the long reign of Uzziah, his son Jotham began his rule in 740 B.C. That was the year the great prophet Isaiah began to preach. And under Jotham was heard yet another prophet—Micah.

Assyria

The Assyrian Empire's renewed military expansion began with extreme violence under Tiglath-pileser III (745-727 B.C.). For a century Assyria was the undisputed power in the entire area. Its power and cultural achievement was at its absolute height. At first Tiglath-pileser repeatedly attacked and defeated the Arameans and Chaldeans, nomadic tribes in the area of Babylonia, sweeping all the way down to the Persian Gulf. After the king of Babylonia died, Tiglath-pileser took over and united the kingdom of Babylonia, adopting a new name, Pulu, for himself, as king of Babylonia.

Then, around 738 B.C., Tiglath-pileser turned against the small kingdoms of Syria, Israel, and Judah. Very soon Syria was paying tribute to Assyria; then it was Israel's turn, during the reign of Menahem.

39 Assyria, to the north and east
of Israel and Judah,
was a strong military power,
with equipment such as
heavy chariots and
battering rams.
The Assyrians were known
for their terror and cruelty.

Assyria was a military state. The king was the commander-in-chief; under him the nobles served as officers commanding armies that were immense for those times. Each spring the Assyrian armies began new offensives. Generally they headed west and crossed the Euphrates River. The soldiers could not swim, but they used inflated goatskins for rafts. They brought along with them horses and heavy-wheeled chariots capable of carrying numerous archers, as well as mules carrying their provisions and tents. They also transported heavy war machines mounted on wheels: battering rams that could demolish the walls of cities under siege.

The courage of the Assyrian soldiers could be glimpsed in such expeditions as those sent against Urartu, in the mountains of Armenia. The soldiers had to make long, difficult marches through forests, ravines, and hills.

The Assyrian methods of warfare were the cruelest found in ancient times. Their aim was to completely terrorize conquered populations and in that way eliminate any thought of rebellion. In cities that had surrendered, any persons trying to resist or rebel in any way were impaled on stakes outside the city gates. If a city did not surrender but had to be conquered, the reprisals were terrible: systematic plunder, massacres of the population and mutilation of the dead, after which the resisting city was burned to the ground. Any surviving people were deported far away to other regions and scattered; conquered populations from elsewhere took their places. It was by such policies that the Assyrians hoped to prevent any uprising in the territories of their vast empire.

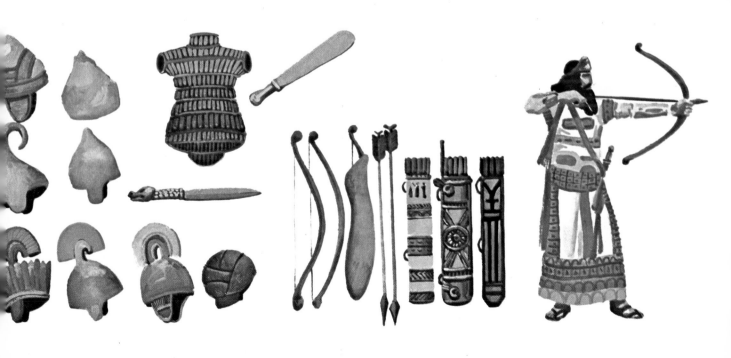

40 The prophet Micah protested against injustice and warned of the fall of both kingdoms. But he also foresaw peace and the restoration of Jerusalem.

The prophet Micah was born in Judah, at Moresheth, a few miles south of Jerusalem. The Book of Micah tells little of his life, only that he prophesied in Judah under Jotham, Ahaz, and Hezekiah, that is, between about 740 and 687 B.C. But his writings give a clear idea of the purpose of his preaching.

The Book of Micah has several great themes. First is the theme of protest against social injustices. Following the example of Amos, who lived a little before him, Micah denounced those people who steal fields and houses, who take property from honest workers, and who cheat in the marketplace with false scales and weights.

Micah saw that even the prophets and priests had become corrupt.

"The city's rulers govern for bribes, the priests interpret the Law for pay, the prophets give their revelations for money—and they all claim that the Lord is with them." (Micah 3:11 TEV)

The just social order desired by God no longer existed.

The second great theme of Micah's preaching was his warning that misfortune would fall upon both Samaria, the capital of the northern kingdom, and upon Jerusalem, the capital of the southern kingdom. His prophetic words about those cities were terrible. Samaria, he said, would end up a pile of rubble, with all its idols smashed. In regard to Jerusalem, he said, "Zion will be plowed like a field, Jerusalem will become a pile of ruins, and the Temple hill will become a forest" (Micah 3:12).

Micah's prophecies were both frightening and ridiculous to those who heard them. "After all," the people told themselves, "no harm will come to us, for the Lord is with us."

Micah continued fearlessly to announce the Lord's severe judgments. He told the people what God wanted from them.

Will the Lord be pleased with thousands
of rams,
with ten thousands of rivers of oil?
Shall I give my first-born for my
transgression,
the fruit of my body for the sin
of my soul?
He has showed you, O man, what is good;
and what does the Lord require of you
but to do justice, and to love kindness,
and to walk humbly with your God?
(Micah 6:7-8)

The third great theme in the Book of Micah is the theme of hope in the salvation of God. This salvation was tied to a renewal of the Law and to respect for the word of God. If only these things could come about, Jerusalem would be restored. Jerusalem

would become the center of the world, towards which peoples from everywhere would stream to hear the word of God. Here is Micah's prophecy of hope:

"In days to come
the mountain where the Temple stands
will be the highest one of all,
towering above all the hills.
Many nations will come streaming to it,
and their people will say,
'Let us go up the hill of the Lord,
to the Temple of Israel's God.
For he will teach us what he
wants us to do;
we will walk in the paths he has chosen.

For the Lord's teaching comes
from Jerusalem;
from Zion he speaks to his people.'

He will settle disputes among the nations,
among the great powers near and far.
They will hammer their swords into plows
and their spears into pruning knives.
Nations will never again go to war,
never prepare for battle again.
Everyone will live in peace
among his own vineyards and fig trees,
and no one will make him afraid.
The Lord Almighty has promised this."

(Micah 4:1-4 TEV)

41 The Book of Isaiah
probably was written
by three different prophets
at three different times.
The first prophet, Isaiah,
(for whom the book is named)
wrote during the reigns
of four kings of Judah.
It was through a vision
in the Temple that God
called Isaiah to be a prophet.
From then on, Isaiah
was overcome by
God's glory and
his own mission.

One of the greatest prophets in the tradition of Amos, Hosea, and Micah was the prophet Isaiah. Son of Amoz, Isaiah was born around 760 B.C., and he carried out his prophetic mission for over forty years under four kings of Judah: Uzziah, Jotham, Ahaz, and Hezekiah.

Isaiah was married to a woman who was herself a prophetess; they had two children. Probably Isaiah was some kind of advisor or counselor to the king, since he seems to have been able to present himself at court at any time without asking permission from anybody. This fact has led many to believe that Isaiah was of noble origin, perhaps even related to the royal family, but there is no proof for this.

What is certain about the prophet, however, is that he was very well educated. Of all the prophets known to us, he was surely the most gifted as a writer. His words contain rich images, great sharpness of language, and expressive comparisons—all of which make his writing stand out in biblical literature, as well as in world literature in general.

Isaiah's personality was strange and fascinating; a whole school of prophetic thought and expression imitated and followed him. In fact, the book of the Bible that bears his name was not written entirely by him alone. Disciples of this great prophet later enriched and added to his work. Modern study of the Bible has identified three different authors of the Book of Isaiah. Chapters 1 to 39 were composed by the prophet Isaiah. Chapters 40 to 55 are by an author who wrote later, around the year 540 B.C., during the Babylonian exile; scholars call him Second Isaiah. Finally, Chapters 56 to 66 are considered the work of a prophet who wrote about 400 B.C.; scholars call him Third Isaiah.

Isaiah, the original prophet of the eighth century, probably had already experienced some prophetic inspiration from God before the year 740. However, as Isaiah himself says, that year an extraordinary event transformed his whole life. He had a vision in which he saw the throne of God suspended in the heavens; the magnificent train of God's robe filled the entire Temple. Around God's throne, seraphim chanted,

"Holy, holy, holy is the Lord of hosts;
the whole earth is full of his glory."

(Isaiah 6:3)

The Temple filled with smoke. The prophet, who had glimpsed the glory of heaven for only an instant, felt himself overcome by the presence of God. This presence suddenly revealed to Isaiah his own unworthiness. He cried out,

"Woe is me! For I am lost;
for I am a man of unclean lips."

(Isaiah 6:5)

Then one of the seraphim took a burning coal from the heavenly altar. He flew towards the prophet and touched and purified his lips with the burning coal. From then on, Isaiah was worthy to proclaim the word of God.

This splendid vision was at the heart of all the prophetic activity of Isaiah. It impressed upon him forever a sense of the glory of God and also of the importance of his mission. A prophet is one sent by God to proclaim his word to the people—the words uttered by the prophet are God's words.

42 Syria and Israel,
both controlled by Assyria,
attacked Judah.
Isaiah urged King Ahaz
to trust in the Lord.
Instead, Ahaz sought help
from Assyria.

The reign of Tiglath-pileser III of Assyria was a turning point in the history of Israel and Judah. First the Assyrian king succeeded in wiping out all internal opposition in his own kingdom, and then he conquered Babylonia. After that, he started a campaign of military expansion that very soon put an end to the northern kingdom of Israel, and brought the southern kingdom of Judah into submission to Assyria.

But just before the final clash with Assyria, there was a small war in which the two Jewish kingdoms opposed each other on the battlefield. At that time, Israel was already a vassal state to Assyria; Syria, too, was forced to pay heavy tribute to Nineveh, the capital of Assyria. In the year 734 B.C. Tiglath-pileser was heavily involved in troubles in the eastern part of his empire. The idea occurred to Rezin, the king of Syria, and to Pekah, the king of Israel, to join together to try to throw off Assyrian domination. In order to succeed, this new alliance between Israel and Syria required help from as many as possible of the neighboring small kingdoms. For this reason even Ahaz, the king of Judah, was invited to join the alliance.

Ahaz, however, declined to join. The kings of Israel and Syria decided to march against Ahaz, depose him, and put a more determined anti-Assyrian king on the throne of Judah.

To protect Judah, King Ahaz set to work to improve the fortifications of Jerusalem; he also

thought about sending messengers to seek help from Assyria. It was while the king was inspecting the fortifications of the city that the prophet Isaiah presented himself to him. Isaiah brought him a message from the Lord: The anger of the kings of Israel and Syria were nothing but the smoke from "two smoldering sticks of wood" (Isaiah 7:4 TEV). Judah should trust in the Lord; only the Lord could save Judah against them anyway. With the Lord there was no need for Ahaz to fear either Rezin, the king of Syria, or Pekah, the king of Israel. Nor was there any need to send messengers to ask the king of Assyria for help.

King Ahaz did not heed the words of the prophet Isaiah. Not only did he send messengers to the king of Assyria; he also plundered the gold and silver treasures from the Temple in order to send gifts to him through these messengers.

It is not known whether Ahaz's messengers or gifts made any difference. Probably Tiglath-pileser was already on the march against the two rebel kings. At any rate, the Assyrian king decisively defeated Rezin and Pekah in the year 733 B.C.— well before they could reach Jerusalem. Syria was made an Assyrian province, and so was the northern part of Israel. Many of the people of Syria and Israel were deported.

At that point, Pekah's subjects rebelled and killed him, probably with the agreement of the Assyrian authorities. A man named Hoshea was put on the throne in his place; he was destined to be the last king of Israel. Hoshea quickly paid homage to Tiglath-pileser, and he was allowed to keep the area around Samaria—from the Plain of Jezreel to the border with Judah.

The Assyrian king then moved against Judah. King Ahaz could console himself that Jerusalem was spared, but his kingdom was penetrated by Assyrian troops, and part of it became subject to Tiglath-pileser.

43 Isaiah wrote about
a vineyard lovingly cared for
by its owner.
But when it bore no fruit,
the owner wanted to abandon it.
"Israel is the vineyard
of the Lord; the people of Judah
are the vines he planted."

Listen while I sing you this song,
  a song of my friend and his vineyard:
My friend had a vineyard
  on a very fertile hill.
He dug the soil and cleared it of stones;
  he planted the finest vines.
He built a tower to guard them,
  dug a pit for treading the grapes.
He waited for the grapes to ripen,
  but every grape was sour.

So now my friend says, "You people who live in Jerusalem and Judah, judge between my vineyard and me. Is there anything I failed to do for it? Then why did it produce sour grapes and not the good grapes I expected?

"Here is what I am going to do to my vineyard: I will take away the hedge around it, break down the wall that protects it, and let wild animals eat it and trample it down. I will let it be overgrown with weeds. I will not trim the vines or hoe the ground; instead, I will let briers and thorns cover it. I will even forbid the clouds to let rain fall on it."

Israel is the vineyard of the Lord Almighty;
  the people of Judah are the vines he planted.
He expected them to do what was good,
  but instead they committed murder.
He expected them to do what was right,
  but their victims cried out for justice.
               (Isaiah 5:1-7 TEV)

Isaiah's words are about the generous mercy of God, as contrasted with the ingratitude and wickedness of human beings.

This writing can be divided into three parts: 1) a word picture of the loving care God lavishes on his vineyard, as he does all in his power to make the vineyard yield good grapes; 2) a call to the people to judge for themselves the poor yield from the vineyard; and 3) God's just decision simply to get rid of the poor-yielding vineyard and stop caring for it.

The vineyard, of course, stands for the people of Judah, who have failed to respond to God's care. So God will abandon his people, just as a winegrower might abandon a vineyard that does not yield.

Isaiah's words begin with celebrating God's mercy and love, and they end on something of a threatening note. However, just as no winegrower is really likely to abandon his vineyard forever, so God will again concern himself in the affairs of the people. Once God's anger has passed, God will again lavish loving care upon the people.

44 In 722 B.C., Assyria
captured Samaria,
the capital of Israel.
This was the end of the
northern kingdom.
Upper classes, the rich,
and leaders were deported
and became exiles.
New settlers from other places
mixed with those who remained.

Although God seemed almost hostile towards the people, God's reaction actually showed grief, because the people had turned away. They had broken the covenant which God generously offered. They had refused to listen to the messages continually sent from God through the prophets.

Because of the people's constant rejection, God had no other choice but to abandon the people to their fate—to allow them to undergo the test of suffering in the hope that they would be purified and would later return to God. This is the Bible's explanation for the final and absolute fall of the northern kingdom of Israel in 722 B.C. to the Assyrian king Shalmaneser V, successor of Tiglath-pileser III.

This is how the final collapse of Israel happened: When Tiglath-pileser died in 727 B.C., Hoshea, the

king of Israel, thought he could get out from under Assyria. He stopped paying tribute to Assyria and entered into negotiations with Egypt, a great enemy of Assyria.

Shalmaneser wasted no time at this news. First he had Hoshea arrested. Then he moved to besiege Samaria, Israel's beautiful, luxurious capital. After a siege of around three years, Samaria finally fell in 722 B.C. The actual conquest probably was made under Shalmaneser. It was his successor, Sargon II, however, who organized the conquered territory.

The state of Israel ceased to exist and became an Assyrian province. The conquerers carried out a massive deportation of the people, or, rather, a massive exchange of peoples. The inhabitants of Israel were deported to the northern part of Mesopotamia, near the area inhabited by the Medes. Substituted for them on the territory that formerly was Israel were other conquered people, from Babylonia and various cities in the East.

As had occurred once before, in 733 B.C., this deportation of the people of Israel included especially the upper classes of society; consequently, the remaining population found themselves without government officials, administrators, priests, and so on. A distinct new people emerged around Samaria—a blend of the remaining Israelites and new settlers. They were the Samaritans, who inhabited this same territory during the time of Jesus.

45 Isaiah was a
prophet of hope.
He wrote of a Messiah to come,
a new ruler from David's family,
justice for the helpless,
peace among nations
and in nature,
and the gathering together
again of the exiles.

The Joy of the Redeemed

The people who walked in darkness
　　have seen a great light.
They lived in a land of shadows,
　　but now light is shining on them.
You have given them great joy, Lord;
　　you have made them happy.
They rejoice in what you have done,
　　as people rejoice when they harvest grain
　　or when they divide captured wealth.
For you have broken the yoke that burdened
　　　them
　　and the rod that beat their shoulders.
You have defeated the nation
　　that oppressed and exploited your people,
　　just as you defeated the army of Midian
　　　long ago.
The boots of the invading army
　　and all their bloodstained clothing
　　will be destroyed by fire.
A child is born to us!
　　A son is given to us!
　　And he will be our ruler.
He will be called, "Wonderful Counselor,"
　　"Mighty God," "Eternal Father,"
　　"Prince of Peace." (Isaiah 9:2-6 TEV)

Universal Peace

The royal line of David is like a tree that has been cut down; but just as new branches sprout from a stump, so a new king will arise from among David's descendants.

The spirit of the Lord will give him
　　　wisdom
　　and the knowledge and skill to rule
　　　his people.
He will know the Lord's will and will
　　have reverence for him,
　　and find pleasure in obeying him.
He will not judge by appearance or hearsay;
　　he will judge the poor fairly
　　and defend the rights of the helpless.
At his command the people will be punished,
　　and evil persons will die.
He will rule his people with justice and
　　integrity.

Wolves and sheep will live together
　　in peace,
　　and leopards will lie down with young
　　　goats.
Calves and lion cubs will feed together,
　　and little children will take care of
　　　them.
Cows and bears will eat together,
　　and their calves and cubs will lie down in peace.
Lions will eat straw as cattle do.
Even a baby will not be harmed
　　if it plays near a poisonous snake.
On Zion, God's holy hill,
　　there will be nothing harmful or evil.
The land will be as full of knowledge of
　　　the Lord
　　as the seas are full of water.

A day is coming when the new king from the royal line of David will be a symbol to the nations. They will gather in his royal city and give him honor. When that day comes, the Lord will once again use his power and bring back home those of his people who are left in Assyria and Egypt, in the lands of Pathros, Sudan, Elam, Babylonia, and Hamath, and in the coastlands and on the islands of the sea. The Lord will raise a signal flag to show the nations that he is gathering together again the scattered people of Israel and Judah and bringing them back from the four corners of the earth. (Isaiah 11:1-12 TEV)

46 Hezekiah, king of Judah
after Israel fell,
restored the Temple as center
for the worship of God.
Priests and people rededicated
themselves to the covenant.

The end of the kingdom of Israel did not mean any change for the kingdom of Judah. King Ahaz continued his policy of submitting to Assyria; he even allowed some objects of Assyrian worship to be placed in the Temple, as the Assyrians wished. He did this in spite of God's command to have no other god in his presence. In this way, Judah managed to remain a small, self-governing territory within the Assyrian Empire.

Hezekiah, the son of Ahaz, became king in 716 B.C., and began a different policy. Advised by the prophet Isaiah, Hezekiah began a basic religious reform within the kingdom.

First of all, he had the Temple cleansed, reconsecrated, and restored to its position as the national center of worship. The Assyrian worship objects were removed. Hezekiah summoned all the priests and Levites to Jerusalem. They dedicated themselves to God and promised to be faithful in their duties and responsibilities. Hezekiah thought that if the priests lived and acted according to regular rules, there would be a better chance to keep the worship of God free of the abuses of the past.

At the same time, Hezekiah provided the priests with the income necessary for their support. According to the ancient tradition, the support of the priests and the Levites was to come through a tithe, or ten percent religious tax on income. Following Hezekiah's reforms, the offerings to the Temple were more than sufficient, and the surplus was stored in the rooms of the Temple. After having provided for the priests, Hezekiah organized a solemn ceremony of purification for them and had it celebrated in his presence.

Hezekiah knew that his people had a great need to be confirmed in their faith, so the king and his counselors revived the long-neglected festival of the Passover. They decided that this feast should be solemnly celebrated in Jerusalem, where the central sanctuary of the Hebrew religion, the Temple, was located.

So Hezekiah sent out messengers to the surrounding countryside, not only in Judah itself but even in some of the territories of the vanished kingdom of Israel. This is the only case known of the Hebrews of Judah attempting to re-establish contact with whatever brothers and sisters of theirs remained in the northern territories. The results were not very encouraging. Only a few scattered members of the tribes of Asher, Manasseh, and Zebulon responded to this invitation from the king of Judah to come to Jerusalem to worship.

Within Judah itself, however, King Hezekiah's call for the renewal of the worship of God was received with nearly unanimous acclaim. The inhabitants of the country began coming to Jerusalem yearly to celebrate the Passover for one entire week,

following to the letter the prescriptions of Moses.

As part of this renewal of the covenant, Hezekiah worked to eliminate all foreign idols and the sanctuaries where they were worshiped. In this way, Hezekiah's religious reform was completed. The Hebrew people in Judah once again officially affirmed their covenant with the God of Abraham, Isaac, and Jacob.

Hezekiah's concerns, however, were not solely religious. He repeatedly refused to enter into the various alliances and coalitions that were formed in resistance to Assyrian power; but he realized that sooner or later he would probably have to face the Assyrian king. So he carried out extensive preparations to defend Jerusalem. He had a number of underground canals dug to ensure a water supply to the city in case of siege. He rebuilt the walls of Jerusalem and added defensive towers. Finally, he reorganized his army and provided it with adequate weapons. He knew Judah's army could not actually compete with Assyria's, but at least it could defend the kingdom for a period of time.

47 Against the advice of Isaiah,
King Hezekiah sought
various alliances against Syria.
Isaiah's message was
"Trust in God.
Alliances will not save you."

"In quietness and trust shall be your strength" (Isaiah 30:15). These words of the prophet sum up what he thought should be Judah's attitude towards neighboring powers. For a long period of time, King Hezekiah followed the prophet's advice, and he stayed clear of entangling alliances. In the year 705 B.C., however, he himself organized a new alliance, aimed at freeing Syria, Judah, and other small kingdoms east of the Jordan from the control of the Assyrians. Hezekiah's reasons for this change in foreign policy are not known. Probably Hezekiah hoped to take advantage of a change of rulers in Assyria at that time. At that time he already was in alliance with Egypt and the Philistine cities of Ashkelon and Ekron, as well as with some other small kingdoms in the area.

Whatever his reasons were, at a certain point the king of Judah refused any longer to pay tribute to the Assyrians in Nineveh. Sargon II had been succeeded on the throne of Assyria by his son Sennacherib. Because the new ruler's first task was to firmly establish his power in the East, for three years Sennacherib was not able to march westward.

The weakness of the anti-Assyrian alliance soon became clear. The other small kingdoms gave in without a fight, or resisted only briefly. Egypt still remained; however, as Isaiah had always predicted, Egypt was really not able to fight Assyrian power.

And so the kingdom of Judah found itself all alone in the face of a large Assyrian army. After first having captured nearly fifty other Judean towns, the army had come to besiege Jerusalem. In some words of Sennacherib's that have come down to us, Hezekiah was "imprisoned in Jerusalem, his residence, like a bird in its cage." That is why the eventual outcome of this siege is so surprising.

In accord with their usual military practice, the Assyrians offered the inhabitants of Jerusalem a

chance to surrender. There were frantic consultations inside the city. Then a delegation went out to negotiate with Sennacherib. But the Assyrians taunted the people, asking them if it made sense to rely on their God, since the gods of all the other peoples conquered by Assyria, including Israel, had failed to save them.

Frightened and despairing, Hezekiah turned to Isaiah. Isaiah encouraged the people to stand firm and resist the Assyrians:

"Thus says the Lord concerning the king of Assyria, He shall not come into this city or shoot an arrow there. . . . By the way that he came, by the same shall he return, and he shall not come into this city, says the Lord." (2 Kings 19:32-33)

The outcome was just as Isaiah had predicted. At dawn one morning the Assyrians withdrew in great disorder. Perhaps a sudden sickness struck the Assyrian camp; or perhaps the king of Assyria received word of a threat in another part of his empire. But whatever the reason was, the Assyrians lifted their seige and Jerusalem was not captured.

Hezekiah did have to pay a price for joining the anti-Assyrian alliance, however; parts of his territory were occupied and some of his people taken away, and he also had to pay a greater tribute to Assyria.

Another incident between King Hezekiah and Isaiah occurred after the visit of a Babylonian delegation. The delegation brought gifts for Hezekiah, who had made something of a name for himself as an opponent of the Assyrians. Flattered by this attention, the king conducted the Babylonian delegation on a tour to show off his royal palace and all its treasures.

The Babylonian delegation had barely departed when Isaiah appeared before Hezekiah. He learned what the king had done and then scolded him severely for it. Isaiah prophesied that all the king's treasures would eventually be carried off to Babylonia; by trying to impress the Babylonians, Hezekiah had shown a lack of trust in God. Isaiah warned Hezekiah:

"Hear the word of the Lord: Behold the days are coming, when all that is in your house, and that which your fathers have stored up till this day, shall be carried to Babylon; nothing shall be left, says the Lord." (2 Kings 20:16-17; Isaiah 39:5-6)

Up to the very end Isaiah did not change his basic message: Trust in God and not in the powers of this world.

48
After finding "The Book
of the Law" in the Temple,
King Josiah led a renewal
of Judah's covenant with God.
He tried to purge the nation
of the worship of idols,
and executed the priests who
worshiped at pagan altars.
He restored the Temple
as a national center of worship.

The Bible provides us with many details about happenings late in the reign of Hezekiah, who died in 687 B.C. But from then up to the religious reforms of King Josiah in 622 B.C. few historical details are provided. During all these years, Judah remained a vassal state of Assyria. Meanwhile, important changes were taking place on the world scene.

Assyria had reached the height of its power and domination around 670 B.C. when it conquered Egypt. Then quite rapidly it grew weaker, due to internal difficulties. The Babylonians began to grow strong as a people, threatening to take Assyria's place as a power, with the help of the Medes, a tribe that inhabited northern Persia. Also Egypt had recovered its independence, and by Josiah's time it was again a strong state.

It is necessary to understand these world changes in order to understand the reign of Josiah. Josiah was the last king of Judah who had a grand and imaginative plan of rule; he hoped to profit from developments in the international field, not only to liberate Judah from the Assyrians, but also to extend his kingdom northwards into the territory of the former kingdom of Israel.

Following the example of Hezekiah, Josiah's first major move was a religious one. He gave orders for a restoration of the Temple. During the work on the Temple, the high priest Hilkiah found "the Book of the Law" within the Temple. This book, containing a series of religious laws and directions, had probably been brought to Jerusalem by fleeing refugees at the time of the fall of Samaria. Later this book came to be called by the Greek word *Deuteronomy*, which means "second law."

This book deeply impressed King Josiah; he decided to begin a complete religious reform. He invited representatives of the people to Jerusalem. In the presence of all the priests, Levites, elders, and prophets, he had read to the assembled crowd the entire Book of the Law that had been discovered in the Temple. Standing by the pillar reserved for him, he solemnly renewed the covenant of God with all the people, in accordance with the directions contained in the Book of Deuteronomy.

After the covenant renewal, Josiah ordered a complete and careful purification of the whole land. Pagan altars and sanctuaries were destroyed; idols and pillars were broken in pieces. Josiah had priests of these idolatrous cults executed by burning.

Josiah did not limit his reforms to the kingdom of Judah; he tried to introduce them into the northern territories where Assyrian decline had created something of a vacuum. Josiah not only destroyed the altars of strange foreign gods; he also destroyed the sanctuaries of the God of Israel. In this way, Josiah tried to emphasize the uniqueness of the Temple; only in the building constructed by Solomon could God be worshiped in his fullness. Destruction of sanctuaries of all kinds was also a precaution against a revival of idolatry, a very real possibility during those confused times. Many years later, Jesus would declare that it was possible to "worship the Father in spirit and truth" wherever one happened to be (John 4:23), but that time was still to come.

49

The prophet Zephaniah warned of "the day of the Lord," when everything would be blown away like chaff in the wind. About 700 B.C. editors started to combine written traditions from Israel and Judah. Later these traditions would become part of Scripture.

Although Hezekiah saved Jerusalem from the Assyrians' siege, Judah remained subject to Assyria for the rest of Hezekiah's reign, as well as during the reigns of his son Manasseh and grandson Amon. Manasseh during his long reign of forty-five years did a great deal to support the Assyrians' religion. Considered by many to be Judah's worst king, he reopened pagan shrines and altars, allowed human sacrifice, and even placed pagan statues inside the Temple and its courtyard.

The worship of pagan gods was still common in Judah in the early years of the reign of Josiah, Manasseh's grandson. And it was during those years that the prophet Zephaniah began to speak.

In the short Book of Zephaniah, the prophet denounced the paganism that had spread throughout Judah: the cult of the stars from Assyria; the cult of Baal from Phoenicia, and the cult of the god Milcom from the Ammonites. All these pagan practices had become mixed up with the worship of the true God. Zephaniah preached the coming of "the day of the Lord"—a time when a disaster would overturn everything and blow it away like chaff in the wind. The pagans would be punished, but Jerusalem would also be punished for its lack of faith. Zephaniah also prophesied the fall of Nineveh, the Assyrian capital, and the total destruction of power of Assyria, which had oppressed Judah for more than a century.

However, Jerusalem would be converted as a result of being punished, according to Zephaniah; she would again rejoice in the Lord:
"Do not fear, O Zion;
  let not your hands grow weak.
The Lord, your God, is in your midst,
  a warrior who gives victory;
he will rejoice over you with gladness,
  he will renew you in his love."
(Zephaniah 3:16-17)

It was after Zephaniah's preaching that the Book of Deuteronomy was discovered in the Temple during reconstruction work ordered by King Josiah. Bible scholars have explained the origin of this book in several ways. Some scholars think this law book was written by prophets who escaped to Jerusalem after the northern kingdom fell to the Assyrians in 722 B.C.

The Book of Deuteronomy is the first in a collection of writings that includes Joshua, Judges, and Kings. This collection is called the Deuteronomic tradition.

Another biblical tradition which came from the northern tribes is the Elohist tradition, so-called because the author of these writings in Hebrew referred to God as *Elohim*. This tradition included stories of Abraham, the other patriarchs, and Moses—as those stories were preserved by the northern tribes. At some point in the Elohist document's history, ancient texts of the law—the Ten Commandments and Covenant Code (Exodus 20-23)—were added to its narrative.

Around 700 B.C. the Elohist document from Israel was compared to the Yahwist tradition (which referred to God as *Yahweh*), which had been written several hundred years earlier in Jerusalem at the time of Solomon. An anonymous editor combined the two documents by adding to the Yahwist tradition those parts of the Elohist writings which seemed appropriate.

The priests of the Temple in Jerusalem preserved and maintained the combined Yahwist-Elohist document. After Jerusalem fell, they took it along to Babylonia. It was the combined Yahwist-Elohist document, along with Deuteronomy and the writings of the prophets, that the Jews would carry with them into exile in Babylon. These writings would help keep alive the faith of the people during that faraway exile.

and replaced Assyria
as the main power
to the east of Judah.
Egypt rushed to aid Assyria.
In 609 B.C. King Josiah
was killed while trying
to defend his people
from the Egyptian armies
passing through Judah.

Towards the middle of the seventh century B.C., Assyrian power began to decline. Within about thirty years the end came for Assyria. The first attack came from Nabopolassar, the leader of the Chaldeans, a people originally from the territory around the mouth of the Euphrates River that later had moved into the country around Babylon. Nabopolassar had been able to take over the city of Babylon itself and had had himself proclaimed king of Babylonia in 626 B.C.

During the same period, the Medes under the leadership of their king Cyaxares came down out of the mountains of Persia and settled in the valley of the Tigris. Another people, the Scythians, came out of the steppes north of the Black Sea to settle near the Tigris.

These invasions weakened Assyria. Babylonia, on the other hand, grew stronger, and, eventually, became independent. Finally Cyaxares and Nabopolassar made an agreement and attacked Assyria. The Medes besieged and captured the city of Ashur. The Babylonians did the same to Nineveh and also killed the Assyrian king.

The fall of Nineveh, an all-powerful city only a few years earlier, made a great impression. Nahum, a Hebrew prophet who lived at this time, repeatedly talked about this event in his prophecies. However, even though Assyrian power was greatly weakened, it wasn't completely gone. In Haran in northern Mesopotamia, a man named Ashur-uballit proclaimed himself king of Assyria. Crushed and driven out of the Assyrian capital of Nineveh, he attempted to establish himself in Haran with the help of the Egyptians.

It was surprising for the Egyptians to be aiding the Assyrians, for the two nations were traditional enemies. Assyria had even once invaded Egypt. Now, however, the Egyptians were supporting the Assyrians against the rising power of the Babylonians. They probably wanted the Assyrians to act as a buffer zone between themselves and the Babylonians. So they assisted Ashur-uballit and tried to prop him up in power. They did not succeed in this. In fact, they were themselves defeated and had to withdraw, leaving Babylonia as the dominant power.

Josiah was a victim in one of these constant clashes among the great powers. In 609 B.C. he went out to meet the Egyptian troops marching towards Carchemish on the Euphrates. Probably Josiah wanted to defend his own territories, recently won back from Assyria, and to protect Judah from the effects of being a crossroads for the passage of foreign troops. However, Josiah failed. Pharaoh Neco II defeated and killed him near Megiddo. Josiah's death was a great misfortune for Judah, for the kingdom needed a wise and sure guide.

The Fall of Nineveh
This is a message about Nineveh, the account of a vision seen by Nahum, who was from Elkosh.

The Lord God tolerates no rivals;
 he punishes those who oppose him.
 In his anger he pays them back.
The Lord does not easily become angry,
 but he is powerful
 and never lets the guilty go unpunished.

Where the Lord walks, storms arise;
 the clouds are the dust raised by his feet!

From you, Nineveh, there came a man full of wicked schemes, who plotted against the Lord. This is what the Lord says to his people Israel: "Even though the Assyrians are strong and numerous, they will be destroyed and disappear. My people, I made you suffer, but I will not do it again. I will now end Assyria's power over you and break the chains that bind you." (Nahum 1:1-3, 11-13 TEV)

51 These were the major peoples near Judah around 600 B.C.: Egyptians, Scythians, Babylonians, Medes, Chaldeans.

Black Sea

Scythians. The Scythians originally came from a region north of the Black Sea. Between 630 and 625 B.C., hordes of Scythians descended upon Assyria, Phoenicia, and Palestine; they advanced all the way to the borders of Egypt. Here they were stopped and thrown back by Pharaoh Psammetichus I. Even the king of weakened Assyria, Ashuretililani, was able to push them back from some areas they had overrun.

Scythians

Carchem

Josiah

Mediterranean Sea

Egyptians. Pharaoh Psammetichus I (633-609 B.C.) liberated Egypt from Assyrian domination and began the twenty-sixth dynasty with a capital at Sais in the Nile Delta. His successor Neco II (609-594 B.C.) marched across Palestine to aid the last king of Assyria. At Megiddo, he encountered King Josiah, who attempted to stop him but was instead killed in battle. Neco went on to make himself master of all Syria, but in 605 B.C. he too was defeated by Nebuchadnezzar and pushed back into Egypt.

Megiddo

• **Sais**

Jehoiakim

Egyptians

Babylonians. In 626 B.C. Nabopolassar was able to proclaim himself king of Babylonia. He made an alliance with the Medes; with them he made war on Sinsharishkun, king of Assyria.

Later, in 612 B.C., the city of Nineveh fell under the combined blows of Nabopolassar of Babylon and of Cyaxares, king of the Medes; these two kings were assisted in this by the Scythians. The Assyrian King Sinsharishkun perished amid the flames of his royal palace. The last Assyrian king. Ashur-uballit, tried to hold out in Haran, but he too was defeated in 609 B.C. From then on, Assyria was a Babylonian province.

obligations on them. In 605 B.C. Jehoiakim, the king of Judah, became a vassal of the Babylonians.

In 605 B.C. the Babylonian crown prince, Nebuchadnezzar, defeated Neco II's Egyptian army at Carchemish on the Euphrates; in this way he became overlord of both Syria and Judah. In the same year, Nebuchadnezzar became king of Babylonia himself after his father died. Nebuchadnezzar ruled from 605 to 562 B.C.

Nebuchadnezzar married a daughter of Cyaxares, helping to establish Babylonia's alliance with the Medes. The Medes and the Babylonians then divided up the East. Cyaxares took the northern and eastern parts and made his capital at Ecbatana (Hamadan). Nebuchadnezzar took Assyria, Phoenicia, and Palestine; he tried but failed to conquer Egypt as well.

Nineveh

Haran

Assyria

Syria

Ecbatana

Medes

Babylonia

Chaldeans

Medes. The Medes, who lived in the northern part of Persia, were a people related to the Persians. They were organized into an army by King Cyaxares (625-585 B.C.), and became a great power; they attacked Syria more than once and even conquered part of Asia Minor. Their empire was conquered by the Persians in 550 B.C.

Persian Gulf

After the defeat of Assyria, the Babylonian ruler Nabopolassar and his son Nebuchadnezzar carried on the Assyrian system of collecting tribute from the smaller vassal states. Sometimes they took over territories directly themselves, placing governors over them; other times they allowed local rulers to govern while collecting tribute and imposing other

Chaldeans. The Chaldeans were an Aramean tribe that had settled south of Babylon and around the Persian Gulf. Bolder than the original Babylonians, they had frequently tried to revolt against the Assyrians. In 626 B.C., their leader Nabopolassar became the leader of the strong Babylonian-Medean team that eventually defeated the Assyrians.

52 The great prophet Jeremiah
warned that Babylonia
would soon conquer Judah.
He was ridiculed and persecuted,
but he felt he could not stop
speaking for God.

During the most difficult times in the history of his people, God often sent a prophet. A prophet could speak in God's name, make known his judgments, and, at the same time, encourage the faithful. God's judgments condemning the people were not final; after each punishment there followed a new and more perfect covenant.

The major Hebrew prophet in the last years of Judah was Jeremiah. Just as Isaiah prophesied in the time of Assyrian oppression, so Jeremiah prophesied during the rising power of Babylonia. Jeremiah correctly foretold the fall of Jerusalem.

The prophet Jeremiah was born at Anathoth, about four miles north of Jerusalem. He was the son of the priest Hilkiah. Jeremiah was called to be a prophet around the year 626 B.C., during King Josiah's reign. Jeremiah was shy and did not like confrontation; he was very aware of the great difficulties involved in trying to be a prophet. At one point he prayed to the Lord to excuse him from his mission, pleading that he was too young. The Lord commanded him to carry on, promising to be at his side to protect him from his enemies. And Jeremiah had many enemies, because most of Jeremiah's listeners either did not understand or did not like his message.

After Josiah died, the people of Jerusalem acclaimed his son Jehoahaz as king. After only three months, Jehoahaz was forced from the throne by the Egyptian pharaoh Neco II. Neco named as king the brother of Jehoahaz, whose name was Eliakim. To demonstrate Judah's submission to Egypt, however, Neco made him adopt the name Jehoiakim; he reigned over Judah from 609 to 598 B.C.

These were the years of the prophet Jeremiah's greatest activity as a prophet. He preached against the forms and rituals of organized worship; for him, faith was more personal. God, Jeremiah said, would judge people by what was in their hearts.

Jeremiah also warned about the imminent arrival of the Babylonian conquerers. But since he did this in a country where the king had been placed on the throne by the Egyptian pharaoh and where the pro-Egyptian party was very strong, Jeremiah was not

believed. He was sneered at and people were furious with him. It is not surprising that the prophet soon found himself persecuted, and, finally, even imprisoned.

Jeremiah tried to get out of his difficult mission. He prayed to God to allow him simply to live a peaceful, normal life like those of his neighbors. His efforts to escape were in vain, however; the prophet carried within himself a fire that forced him to proclaim the word of God; more than once the Lord made him understand that prophecy was indeed his mission.

Jeremiah expressed his distress in powerful cries to the Lord. At the end of each outburst, God encouraged the prophet to continue with his mission.

The Mission of the Prophet

What an unhappy man I am! Why did my mother bring me into the world? I have to quarrel and argue with everyone in the land. I have not lent any money or borrowed any; yet everyone curses me. Lord, may all their curses come true if I have not served you well, if I have not pleaded with you on behalf of my enemies when they were in trouble and distress.

Then I said, ''Lord, you understand. Remember me and help me. Let me have revenge on those who persecute me. Do not be so patient with them that they succeed in killing me. Remember that it is for your sake that I am insulted. You spoke to me, and I listened to every word. I belong to you, Lord God Almighty, and so your words filled my heart with joy and happiness. I did not spend my time with other people, laughing and having a good time. In obedience to your orders I stayed by myself and was filled with anger.'' (Jeremiah 15:10-11, 15-17 TEV)

We learn how hard a prophet's life can be from the complaints Jeremiah made to the Lord.

The Word of God Is a Burning Fire

Lord, you have deceived me,
 and I was deceived.
You are stronger than I am,
 and you have overpowered me.
Everyone makes fun of me;
 they laugh at me all day long.
Whenever I speak, I have to cry out
 and shout, ''Violence! Destruction!''
Lord, I am ridiculed and scorned
  all the time
 because I proclaim your message.
But when I say, ''I will forget the Lord
 and no longer speak in his name,''
then your message is like a fire
 burning deep within me.
I try my best to hold it in,
 but can no longer keep it back.
    (Jeremiah 20:7-9 TEV)

53 Jeremiah went to the Temple and warned that the Temple would not protect the people from God's punishment. God was going to destroy even the Temple in which they trusted. God did not want sacrifices but faithfulness to the covenant and justice among the people.

The Lord sent me to the gate of the Temple where the people of Judah went in to worship. He told me to stand there and announce what the Lord Almighty, the God of Israel, had to say to them: "Change the way you are living and the things you are doing, and I will let you go on living here. Stop believing those deceitful words, 'We are safe! This is the Lord's Temple, this is the Lord's Temple, this is the Lord's Temple!'

"Change the way you are living and stop doing the things you are doing. Be fair in your treatment of one another. Stop taking advantage of aliens, orphans, and widows. Stop killing innocent people in this land. Stop worshiping other gods, for that will destroy you. If you change, I will let you go on living here in the land which I gave your ancestors as a permanent possession.

"Look, you put your trust in deceitful words. You steal, murder, commit adultery, tell lies under oath,

offer sacrifices to Baal, and worship gods that you had not known before. You do these things I hate, and then you come and stand in my presence, in my own Temple, and say, 'We are safe!' Do you think that my Temple is a hiding place for robbers? I have seen what you are doing. Go to Shiloh, the first place where I chose to be worshiped, and see what I did to it because of the sins of my people Israel. You have committed all these sins, and even though I spoke to you over and over again, you refused to listen. You would not answer when I called you. And so, what I did to Shiloh I will do to this Temple of mine, in which you trust. Here in this place that I gave to your ancestors and you, I will do the same thing that I did to Shiloh. I will drive you out of my sight as I drove out your relatives, the people of Israel. I, the Lord, have spoken.''

The Lord said, ''Jeremiah, do not pray for these people. Do not cry or pray on their behalf; do not plead with me, for I will not listen to you. Don't you see what they are doing in the cities of Judah and in the streets of Jerusalem? The children gather firewood, the men build fires, and the women mix dough to bake cakes for the goddess they call the Queen of Heaven. They also pour out offerings of wine to other gods, in order to hurt me. But am I really the one they are hurting? No, they are hurting themselves and bringing shame on themselves. And so I, the Sovereign Lord, will pour out my fierce anger on this Temple. I will pour it out on people and animals alike, and even on the trees and the crops. My anger will be like a fire that no one can put out.''
(Jeremiah 7:1-20 TEV)

54 In 597 B.C. Nebuchadnezzar,
king of Babylonia,
captured Jerusalem,
took the king prisoner,
and deported to Babylon
some of the population.

Neco II and Psammetichus to reestablish Egypt as a great empire failed. The Bible comments:

> The King of Egypt did not come again out of his land, for the King of Babylon had taken all that belonged to the King of Egypt, from the Brook of Egypt to the river Euphrates. (2 Kings 24:7)

Once the Babylonians had defeated the Egyptians, they punished those who had favored the Egyptians. Among those was Jehoiakim, king of Judah, who previously had been subjected to paying only a light tribute to Babylonia. And Jehoiakim did something foolish to make the Babylonians even angrier at him.

The fall of Nineveh freed Syria and Palestine of Assyrian domination. The Egyptians were quick to take advantage of this situation, and they in turn imposed their domination over the region, moving all the way north to Carchemish on the Euphrates River. From there they could hold back any new Babylonian advance. This bold move by Egypt succeeded in keeping things as they were for several years. Nabopolassar was old by then and was no longer able to lead his army in battle.

Things changed very rapidly, however, when Nabopolassar's son Nebuchadnezzar took over command of the Babylonian troops. In 605 B.C. he defeated the Egyptians at Carchemish; the Egyptians had to abandon not only Carchemish, but all of Syria and Palestine. Thus the attempts of Pharaohs

Around 600 B.C. Nebuchadnezzar was defeated in an attempt to invade Egypt, and he had to return to Babylon. Taking advantage of this setback for Nebuchadnezzar, Jehoiakim tried to rebel against him. This was a deadly mistake. As soon as enough time had passed to enable him to gather another army, Nebuchadnezzar returned westward again to punish the rebels.

In early 597 B.C., Jehoiakim died, and his son Jehoiachin succeeded him on the throne. But this change of ruler in Judah didn't lessen Nebuchadnezzar's fury. He began a siege of Jerusalem in March of 597, and very soon Jerusalem surrendered to him. Nebuchadnezzar took the king of Judah prisoner, along with all his family and officials. The victors hauled away most of the treasures in the Temple and the royal palace. And following the example of the Assyrians, the Babylonians also deported much of the population of Judah to their capital, Babylon.

Nebuchadnezzar installed as king Zedekiah, an uncle of Jehoiachin's. Just as had happened to the kingdom of Israel, the kingdom of Judah was now drawing towards its end as an independent state; the end would arrive in about ten years.

According to the Bible, the cause of the defeat and exile of Judah lay in the sins of the people, their breaking the law of God. This defeat had been predicted by the prophet Jeremiah. It was also predicted by another prophet of the time—Habakkuk.

The Coming of the Babylonians
"I am bringing the Babylonians to power, those fierce, restless people. They are marching out across the world to conquer other lands. They spread fear and terror, and in their pride they are a law to themselves.

"Their horses are faster than leopards, fiercer than hungry wolves. Their horsemen come riding from distant lands; their horses paw the ground. They come swooping down like eagles attacking their prey.

"Their armies advance in violent conquest, and everyone is terrified as they approach. Their captives are as numerous as grains of sand. They treat kings with contempt and laugh at high officials. No fortress can stop them—they pile up earth against it and capture it. Then they sweep on like the wind and are gone, these men whose power is their god."

(Habakkuk 1:6-11 TEV)

55 Some people in Jerusalem wanted
to rebel against Babylonia.
But Jeremiah believed
this was useless, because
the power of the Babylonians
was part of God's plan.
To symbolize Judah's submission
to the Babylonians,
Jeremiah went to the Temple
with a yoke on his own neck.

In order to have a greater impact with their messages, the prophets sometimes used dramatic symbols along with their words. Jeremiah did this a short time after the Babylonian king Nebuchadnezzar had placed Zedekiah on the throne of Judah and sent the most outspoken opponents of Babylonian domination into exile. Soon after Nebuchadnezzar left Jerusalem, ambassadors began to arrive in Jerusalem from some of the surrounding small kingdoms; their purpose was to get Zedekiah to join them in an alliance organized against Babylonian power. Naturally, some of the remaining Jews were in favor of joining this alliance; they wanted to free themselves from the Babylonians.

In this situation, Jeremiah responded to an inspiration from God, found himself a wooden yoke (a heavy frame used to bind enslaved people or animals) and placed it on his own neck, and then went to the Temple. Through this gesture of wearing a yoke, he was prophesying that soon all the inhabitants of Judah, especially those attempting to resist Babylonia, would fall completely under the Babylonian yoke. Jeremiah explained that this would happen because God, the Creator of the universe, had decreed that for the moment all people should come under the power of the Babylonians; so long as God willed this to be so, rebellion against the Babylonians was useless and would only anger Babylon.

Jeremiah's message contradicted the prophecies of other priests and false prophets in Judah, who were predicting that soon Jerusalem would be liberated and the exiles returned. Jeremiah was in conflict with the official line adopted by the Temple priests. A priest named Hananiah, in particular, reacted violently to Jeremiah's prophecy. Coming upon Jeremiah in the Temple wearing his symbolic yoke, Hananiah declared,

"Thus says the Lord . . . Within two years . . . I will bring back to this place all the vessels of the Lord's house, which Nebuchadnezzar king of Babylon took away from this place and carried to Babylon; I will also bring back . . . all the exiles from Judah who went to Babylon." (Jeremiah 28:2-4)

Then Hananiah walked up to Jeremiah and broke the yoke on his neck. Turning to the people, he announced,

> "Thus says the Lord: Even so will I break the yoke of Nebuchadnezzar king of Babylon from the neck of all the nations within two years."
>
> (Jeremiah 28:11)

Hananiah claimed to be the true prophet and interpreter of the will of God. At the same time he accused Jeremiah of being a false prophet. Jeremiah did not reply immediately. If the words of God did not come to him immediately, he always kept silent. He went away from the Temple, apparently defeated, but a little later God did inspire Jeremiah to reply:

> "Thus says the Lord: You have broken wooden bars, but I will make in their place bars of iron. For thus says the Lord of hosts, the God of Israel: I have put upon the neck of all these nations an iron yoke of servitude to Nebuchadnezzar king of Babylon, and they shall serve him."
>
> (Jeremiah 28:13-14)

Jeremiah continued his prophecy, even announcing the death of Hananiah:

> "Listen, Hananiah, the Lord has not sent you, and you have made this people trust in a lie. Therefore thus says the Lord: 'Behold, I will remove you from the face of the earth. This very year you shall die, because you have uttered rebellion against the Lord.'" (Jeremiah 28:15-16)

This incident between Hananiah and Jeremiah, between the false prophet and the true, teaches an important lesson. The lesson is that one of the greatest temptations of human beings is to ascribe to God, or place in God's mouth, the words that express our own wishes and our own desires. Jeremiah knew, however, that it is always necessary to bear in mind God's wishes and God's commandments, even when they go against our own wishes, hopes, and expectations.

56 Accused of being unpatriotic,
Jeremiah was thrown into prison.
Although he knew that
the end of his nation was near,
Jeremiah had faith in God
and hope for the future.

He bought a field and
carefully stored the contract,
to show that people
would continue to buy
and sell fields and vineyards.

Within just a few years after the clash between Hananiah and Jeremiah, the situation of Judah grew much worse. Zedekiah, the king who had been selected by the Babylonians, let himself be persuaded—or perhaps was forced by the anti-Babylonian party—to rebel against Nebuchadnezzar. The Babylonian army, however, quickly advanced from the north against Zedekiah. Jeremiah continued fearlessly to preach his message: The hoped-for aid from Egypt would not be forthcoming; Jerusalem would fall into the hands of Nebuchadnezzar; Zedekiah and his court would be made prisoners of the Babylonians.

Some of the king's men were not happy to hear such preaching, so they went to Zedekiah and demanded that Jeremiah be punished.

"Let this man be put to death, for he is weakening the hands of the soldiers who are left in this city, and the hands of all the people, by speaking such words to them." (Jeremiah 38:4)

Jeremiah was thus accused of weakening the people's spirit of resistance. Zedekiah, a weak man, did not have the courage to oppose his advisors, and he did not have the courage to execute the prophet. So he had Jeremiah imprisoned in the court of the guard, a lesser punishment. And, from time to time, the king even continued to consult him secretly.

It was during this period while he was imprisoned in the court of the guard that Jeremiah did something meant to give hope to his people, who were frightened by the Babylonian threat. When his cousin, Hanamel, visited him in prison and suggested that he buy a field in Anathoth, his native village located a few miles outside Jerusalem, Jeremiah agreed. He sent for his secretary, Baruch, and had a contract for the sale drawn up, observing every detail of the law. He signed the contract in the presence of two witnesses and paid his cousin with two pieces of silver carefully weighed on the scales. Then he ordered Baruch to put the signed contract in a terracotta vase and keep it in a safe place.

By doing this, Jeremiah wanted to instill some confidence in the future amidst the general hopelessness of the people. Jerusalem would be captured and destroyed, but even that would not be the end of the world—life would go on.

"The people are saying that this land will be like a desert where neither people nor animals live, and that it will be given over to the Babylonians. But fields will once again be bought in this land. People will buy them, and the deeds will be signed, sealed, and witnessed. This will take place in the territory of Benjamin, in the villages around Jerusalem, in the towns of Judah, and in the towns in the hill country, in the foothills, and in southern Judah. I will restore the people to their land. I, the Lord, have spoken."

(Jeremiah 32:43-44 TEV)

In other words, in the end life would win out over violence, destruction, and death.

57 After a rebellion by Judah, in 587 B.C., the Babylonians completely destroyed Jerusalem. The kingdom of Judah was no more.

In 589 B.C. the kingdom of Judah rebelled against the Babylonians. We do not know why Zedekiah took this final, fatal step. Perhaps the king was pushed into it by his advisors. Probably they were influenced by anti-Babylonian uprisings in Tyre and Sidon, and perhaps also by promises of help from the new Egyptian pharaoh, Psammetichus II. But whatever the reason, in 589 B.C. Zedekiah refused to pay the required tribute to Babylon, and, in the same year, Babylonian troops invaded the territory of Judah.

The Bible does not give many details about the end of David's kingdom. But in 1935, archeologists dug up evidence related to this Babylonian campaign; these were some writings called "the Lachish letters." These letters provide information about the advance of the Babylonian troops. Lachish was the last fortified city of Judah before Jerusalem itself; the commander of Judah's army must have maintained his headquarters there.

One of the letters read as follows: "My lord should know that we are watching and following the signals from Lachish given out by your lordship, because we can no longer see the signals from Azekah." This letter was undoubtedly sent from some point between Lachish and Azekah. The soldiers there could still see the signals from Lachish but not from Azekah, where the Babylonians had already arrived. About this, the Bible comments,

The king of Babylon was fighting against Jerusalem and against all the cities of Judah that were left, Lachish and Azekah; for these were the only fortified cities of Judah that remained.

(Jeremiah 34:7)

These indications give us some idea of the defense organized by King Zedekiah. Closed up in fortified cities, the Jews communicated by means of signals,

probably making use of fire, and, when possible, by messengers.

It was all in vain. The Babylonian army reached the outskirts of Jerusalem in 589 B.C. and laid siege to the city in an ever-tightening vise. The siege lasted two years. At the end of 587 B.C. it became apparent that the city would have to surrender within a couple of months. Probably the Babylonian siege was not completely continuous during those two years. When we consider that during the earlier siege of 597 B.C. Jerusalem held out for only a couple of months, the city's resistance on this occasion seems amazing. Jeremiah informs us, however, that an Egyptian army at one point made preparations to provide help to the Jews. This might have forced the Babylonians to interrupt their operations temporarily, but it did not mean the end of the war, as many of the Jews had hoped and expected.

In 587 B.C., then, the Babylonians returned again in force, and they reduced the population of Jerusalem to famine conditions. Finally they breached the walls and entered Jerusalem. Zedekiah and his closest advisors fled by night, but they were pursued and captured near Jericho. The king and his sons were carried off by Nebuchadnezzar to Riblah in central Syria, and there they were tortured horribly.

Meanwhile, Jerusalem itself was sacked and almost completely destroyed. The golden furnishings and trimmings of the Temple were carried off; so were its bronze columns and a huge bronze basin. Then, by order of Nebuchadnezzar, the Temple, the royal palace, and the city walls were razed to the ground. Jerusalem, in effect, no longer existed; in the words of the prophet, it was reduced to a heap of rubble.

Nevertheless, the misfortunes of the Jews were far from being over. Those who had actively supported the rebellion were killed; all government officials, scribes, and priests were chained together and deported to Babylonia. Left in Judah were only the lowest classes of the population—artisans and farmers; they were left in the charge of a man named Gedaliah.

From all appearances, the history of the Chosen People was ended; from all appearances, God had failed to keep the promises made to Abraham, Moses, and David. However, God remained faithful to his people; and, after a time of purification, God would bring them back to himself.

58 Jerusalem and the Temple
were destroyed.
Many Israelites were taken
into exile in Babylon.
Yet Jeremiah believed that
God would turn mourning
into joy
and would not reject his people.
They would return to Jerusalem.
God would make a new covenant
and write his law
on their hearts.

"I Will Turn Their Mourning into Joy"

The Lord says, "The time is coming when I will be the God of all the tribes of Israel, and they will be my people. In the desert I showed mercy to those people who had escaped death. When the people of Israel longed for rest, I appeared to them from far away. People of Israel, I have always loved you, so I continue to show you my constant love. Once again I will rebuild you. Once again you will take up your tambourines and dance joyfully. Once again you will plant vineyards on the hills of Samaria, and those who plant them will eat what the vineyards produce. Yes, the time is coming when watchmen will call out on the hills of Ephraim, 'Let's go up to Zion, to the Lord our God.'"

The Lord says,
"Sing with joy for Israel,
    the greatest of the nations.
Sing your song of praise,
    'The Lord has saved his people;
    he has rescued all who are left.'
I will bring them from the north
    and gather them from the ends of the earth.
The blind and the lame will come with them,
    pregnant women and those about to give birth.
They will come back a great nation.
My people will return weeping,
    praying as I lead them back.
I will guide them to streams of water,
    on a smooth road where they will not
        stumble.
I am like a father to Israel
    and Ephraim is my oldest son."

The Lord says,
"Nations, listen to me
    and proclaim my words on the far-off shores.
I scattered my people, but I will gather them
    and guard them as a shepherd guards his flock.
I have set Israel's people free
    and have saved them from a mighty nation.
They will come and sing for joy on Mount Zion
    and be delighted with my gifts—
    gifts of grain and wine and olive oil,
    gifts of sheep and cattle.
They will be like a well-watered garden;
    they will have everything they need.
Then the girls will dance and be happy,
    and men, young and old, will rejoice.
I will comfort them and turn their mourning into joy,
    their sorrow into gladness.
I will fill the priests with the richest food
    and satisfy all the needs of my people.
I, the Lord, have spoken."

(Jeremiah 31:1-14 TEV)

A New Heart

The Lord says, "The time is coming when I will make a new covenant with the people of Israel and with the people of Judah. It will not be like the old covenant that I made with their ancestors when I took them by the hand and led them out of Egypt. Although I was like a husband to them, they did not keep that covenant. The new covenant that I will make with the people of Israel will be this: I will put my law within them and write it on their hearts. I will be their God, and they will be my people. None of them will have to teach his fellow countryman to know the Lord, because all will know me, from the least to the greatest. I will forgive their sins and I will no longer remember their wrongs. I, the Lord, have spoken." (Jeremiah 31:31-34 TEV)

59 Over the years, the prophets spoke often to the Chosen People about their relationships with God and one another.

The Temple. For the people of Israel the Temple was the symbol of God's presence. They even began to think of it as an almost magical object which by itself would protect Jerusalem from enemy attacks.

Prophets, especially Jeremiah and Ezekiel, kept telling the people that only a sincere turning to God and faithfulness to God's law could really save the city and the nation. If the people would not turn back to God, God would allow even the Temple to be destroyed.

The Covenant of Sinai. The basic commitment under the covenant of Sinai was faith in the One God: "You shall have no other gods before me" (Exodus 20:3). Often the people broke the covenant because of the superstitious notion that the false gods would help them.

The prophets' main task was calling the people to obey the covenant and to turn away from worshiping idols. The prophets warned the people that God would punish them for their unfaithfulness and reward them for their faithfulness.

Social Protest. In a society made up primarily of farmers and shepherds, detailed law codes (Exodus 20, 22-23, 33) told the people how they were to live justly. There was a fundamental concern for protecting the most defenseless members of society: the poor, widows, orphans, and strangers in the land.

Later on, in the time of the prophets, social structures became more complicated, and the gap between rich and poor grew. The prophets protested loudly against the pride and display of wealth by the rich. They condemned the mistreatment of the poor and helpless and the shedding of innocent blood through corrupt court decisions and private violence.

Prophets like Amos claimed that external acts of worship and sacrifice were useless as long as injustice continued. The covenant of Sinai required not only faith in the One God but justice among God's people.

The Universal Rule of God. In the teaching of the prophets, God was the Lord of all history. While some of the people persisted in an outworn idea of a national God who would defend the interests of their nation, the prophets believed that God ruled the whole world, Babylon and Assyria as well as Judah and Israel.

One of the tasks of the prophets was to demonstrate how God directed all events—even defeats and national disasters—towards an eventual good

end. In many of the prophetic writings there is a vision of a future in which not only the Chosen People but all peoples will recognize the true God and live together in harmony (Isaiah 2:2-5).

A New Relationship with God. Along with the call to faith in the One God and with the moral and social requirements of the covenant, the prophets preached that it was possible for the Israelites to have a closer, deeper, and more personal relationship with God. First Hosea, and later Jeremiah and Ezekiel, used the image of married love between husband and wife to describe the covenant relationship between God and Israel.

Jeremiah and Ezekiel prophesied a miracle of God to bring about a purer religion in the hearts of his people. Jeremiah described a "New Covenant" in which God would put the law within people and write it on their hearts (Jeremiah 31:31-34). Ezekiel told how God himself would remove their heart of stone and give them a new heart and a new spirit, which would help them to keep his commandments (Ezekiel 36:24-27).

History of Salvation. Some prophets spoke of a "remnant of Israel," a small number of people who survived the disasters befalling the two kingdoms and were faithful to God.

When the northern kingdom fell to the Assyrians, many people were deported; however, some refugees fled to the kingdom of Judah. Judah, along with these added refugees, was known as the "remnant of Israel." Later on the term would be applied to those allowed to return from exile in Babylon to their homeland.

Despite the defeats and difficulties of the Jewish people, the prophets preached that they had a purpose as the Chosen People of God.

True faith was more than an official religion sponsored by the monarchy. During the Babylonian exile the prophets helped the people to understand that the real heart of religion was not ritual or national prosperity, but faithfulness to God. The prophets also gave the people hope that God would send a Messiah from the line of David to establish a kingdom of justice and peace.

Outline by Chapter

KINGS AND PROPHETS

1 Peoples of the Near East
   around 1000 B.C.

2 King Solomon, David's son, asks for wisdom,
   and God makes him a wise and great king

3 Israel's government becomes very well organized,
   and contacts with other nations increase

4 Solomon builds a Temple for God
   and a palace for himself

5 The ark of the covenant,
   the sign of God's presence,
   is brought into the Temple

6 Solomon becomes a strong ruler
   and impresses other nations

7 Israel forgets
   its special relationship to God
   and worships idols from other nations

8 When Solomon dies, his kingdom
   divides into a northern kingdom, Israel,
   and a southern kingdom, Judah

9 Israel worships golden calves;
   instability and rebellion continually
   trouble its rulers

10 Judah, too, is tempted by idolatry;
    Egypt plunders Jerusalem

11 The history of Judah and Israel is a story
    of faithfulness and unfaithfulness to God

12 Usually Judah is more successful
    than Israel in fighting idolatry

13 Omri is one of the few strong rulers
    of Israel, but he, too, worships idols

14 Most neighboring nations think that
    some persons can foretell the future

15 The prophets are special persons
    who speak for God in Israel and Judah

16 The Bible tells many miracle stories
    about Elijah the prophet

17 God's prophet Elijah challenges King Ahab
    and the prophets of Baal to a contest

18 In the contest on Mount Carmel,
    God demonstrates his power

19 In a still, small voice God speaks
    to the discouraged Elijah

20 Elijah confronts Ahab
    after Ahab has murdered Naboth,
    and Elijah predicts Ahab's death

21 Israel contends with Syria,
    a nation to the north

22 Israel defeats the Syrian king, Ben-hadad II

23 Ahab is killed in battle
    against the Syrians

24 Elisha succeeds Elijah and
    continues Elijah's work as God's prophet

25 The Bible tells many miracle stories
    about Elisha the prophet

26 Elisha heals Naaman, a Syrian general,
    of leprosy

27 Syria almost conquers Israel,
    but Israel is saved

28 Elisha anoints a new king, Jehu,
    replacing the wicked family of Ahab

29 Syria and Assyria both threaten Israel
    from the north

30 Jeroboam II is Israel's most powerful king,
    but idolatry and injustice continue

31 The prophet Amos foretells
    the downfall of Israel

32 Amos condemns the luxury of the rich
    and the injustice in Israel

33 The prophet Hosea compares
    Israel to an unfaithful wife

34 Hosea speaks of God's great love
    for his people, despite their unfaithfulness

35 Hosea compares Israel
    to an ungrateful child and
    God to a loving parent

36 Judah has some bad kings
    and also some faithful to God

37 Uzziah is king of Judah
    in a time of prosperity and development